SIGNS AND WONDERS

THE MIRACLES OF GOD

DR. PETE PAWELEK

© 2022 by Pete Pawelek.

All rights reserved.

No part of this publication may be used or reproduced in any manner whatsoever without written permission from the author. No part of this publication may be stored in a retrieval system or transmitted in any form or by any means—electronic, mechanical, photocopying, audio recording, or any other—except for brief quotations in printed reviews, without written permission from the author. The author may be contacted through his website at www.pastorpete.org.

ISBN-13: 9798842344000
Cover design by Marken Media (www.markenmediaco.com)
Interior Design by fiverr.com/mehrangull

Some of the anecdotal illustrations in this book are from real life and are included with the permission of the persons involved. In most cases, specifics that don't alter the meaning of the illustration, such as someone's name, gender, age, and other identifying information, have been changed or removed to protect the actual identity of those mentioned in the book. All other illustrations are composites of real situations, and any resemblance to people living or dead is coincidental.

Unless otherwise identified, all scripture quotations in this publication are taken from the Christian Standard Bible®.

Scripture quotations marked CSB have been taken from the Christian Standard Bible®, copyright© 2017 by Holman Bible Publishers. Used by permission. The Christian Standard Bible® and CSB® are federally registered trademarks of Holman Bible Publishers.
Scripture quotations marked ESV are from the ESV® Bible (The Holy Bible, English Standard Version®), copyright© 2001 by Crossway, a publishing ministry of Good News Publishers. Used by permission. All rights reserved.

If you would like to receive the Daily Devo podcast in your inbox each morning, scan the QR code in the image above or visit www.pastorpete.org to sign up. Each morning, Pastor Pete shares a four-minute devotion with believers from all around the world. Sign up for FREE today!

Dr. Pawelek regularly takes trips to the Holy Land and other spiritually significant locations. If you would like to be notified about future trips use the QR code in the image above or visit www.pastorpete.org. Dr. Pawelek makes these trips as affordable as possible with the purchasing power of large groups. By joining the email list you are *not* signing up for a trip, you are only asking to be notified when trips are planned.

TABLE OF CONTENTS

HIGH FIVES 1
INTRODUCTION 3
EXTRA RESOURCES 7
WEEK ONE: LET'S GET STARTED 11
    War & Walls 15
    Great Honor, Great Hate 19
    Discrete Intentions 23
    Simply Compassion 27
    A Miracle of Grace 31
WEEK TWO: BIBLICAL IDENTIFICATION 37
    Mass Miracles 43
    Manna 47
    Healing & Hatred 51
    Dry Bones 55
    No Answers 59
WEEK THREE: LET'S GET REAL 65
    The Impulse of Faith 69
    Jawbone Hill 73
    Divine Transportation 77
    Earthquakes & Eternity 83
    The Walls Came Down 87
WEEK FOUR: THE SUPERNATURAL 93
    The Robe 97
    Treading on Mercy 101
    Laughing at the Lord 105
    Torn 109

Skin Deep 113
WEEK FIVE: THE PURPOSE **119**
    Never Too Late 123
    Presence, Provision, Protection 127
    The First 131
    Convincingly Unconvinced 135
    Get Up and Go 141
WEEK SIX: WHO PERFORMS MIRACLES? **147**
    Buried by God 151
    Infinite Reach 155
    The Sun Stood Still 159
    An Unwelcome Miracle 163
    A Unique Miracle 167
WEEK SEVEN: MODERN MIRACLES **173**
    A Line in the Sand 177
    God's Sovereignty 181
    Infinite Provision 185
    The Confused Widow 189
    Miracle Machine 193
WEEK EIGHT: COMMON QUESTIONS **199**
    Gruesome & Gladsome 203
    Radical Repentance 207
    Whirlwind of Wonder 211
    Confident in Your Calling 215
    The Miracle of All Miracles 219
WEEK NINE: SMALL GROUP CELEBRATION **225**
APPENDIX A: BIBLICAL SIGNS AND WONDERS **227**

HIGH FIVES

I absolutely love getting and giving high fives. There's just something about slapping hands with others that makes me smile. As I reflect on the completion of this project, there are so many people who deserve high fives for helping me get this project across the finish line.

FAMILY

The first high five is to my family. Each time a new writing project begins, they all know Dad will be in his office and less present in their lives for months. My amazing wife, Abby, graciously puts up with carrying even more of the load at home, allowing me to focus on writing or completing whatever task the Lord has placed on my heart. Without her love, encouragement, and fierce devotion to Jesus, this study would never have been possible. A word of thanks is also in order for my four children. Their curiosity and love for the Lord serve as an eternal spring of inspiration in my life.

FINANCIAL PARTNERS

With self-publishing, so many expenses are required for a project like this. Multiple rounds of editing, proofreading, artwork, cover design, video production, video editing, marketing, and so much more were needed to bring this project to print. A small group of faithful ministry partners made this all possible. They comprise an online group of patrons who contribute monthly to my ministry. Their support makes the Daily Devo podcast and works like this Bible study possible. I would like to offer some special high fives to the following patrons:

J.P.
O.E. Bradshaw
B.W.
Unnamed

If you would like to join our patron community, you can visit my website www.pastorpete.org or use this QR code below to learn more.

FRIENDS

I would like to give just a few more high fives to my friends who spent time reviewing this work and offering their insights and encouragement about the manuscript along the way. This work was enhanced greatly through the revisions I made based on these friends' suggestions. Thank you for taking the time to help me with this project. And, even more importantly, thank you for being my friends.

Clif Jones	**Dr. Ron Dudley**	**Chris Strick**
Andrew Bolt	**Pam Hughes**	**Dr. Paul McQuerry**
Brandon Blasingame	**Ashley Walpole**	**Billy Reed**
Tiffany McKinley	**Larry Castro**	**Mike Romero**
Rachel Hance	**Heather Kahl**	

PROFESSIONAL SERVICES

Finally, I would like to thank my friends at Marken Media for using their gifts in the areas of marketing, artwork, and video production for this project. Their work is amazing and their hearts are on fire for the Kingdom of God. Visit them at www.markenmediaco.com

INTRODUCTION

WHAT THIS STUDY IS

Like many people, I have always been fascinated with God's signs and wonders. Growing up in a conservative evangelical environment, I heard about the miracles of God in church, at camp, and later during my seminary studies. There was, however, always a feeling of suspicion and uneasiness around the subject. Most of the sermons I have heard (and preached myself) over the years tend to focus on the details of the miracle. The few Bible studies I have been a part of that dared to tackle God's signs and wonders either spent most of their efforts trying to explain them away or expanded their scope and significance to the point I considered to be biblically unreasonable. So, when I was encouraged to develop this Bible study, I wanted it to be different. I wanted to offer something that I felt was missing when it comes to understanding God's signs and wonders.

As I have researched, considered, and prayed over the miraculous events contained in the Bible, I'm aware that the complexity of the subject is undeniable. However, it is very easy to dive so deep into the details of these events that their intended message becomes overcomplicated. Therefore, I have labored extensively to keep things as simple as possible in this study. In my experience, it is easy to miss the message because as observers we become too focused on the miracle itself. I believe that the miracles we see in Scripture were not intended to be difficult to understand or even remotely mysterious. Rather, they are a manifestation of the power and glory of God for all to see. Therefore, we should first and foremost look at these events through the lens of simplicity and attempt to understand them as if we were there when they occurred.

Please note that this work is designed to be a Bible study, not a book you read from cover to cover. If you're looking for a book you can just pick up and read to uncover all of the answers to your questions about miracles, then you'll be disappointed. The power of this study emerges when you open your Bible and join the Holy Spirit on a journey into the miraculous. I firmly believe that it is the words contained in Scripture—far more than the words contained in the pages of this study—that will impact your life the most. This is a Bible study that is best experienced with a group of other faithful believers.

WHAT THIS STUDY IS NOT

Any time a writer attempts to tackle a subject like God's signs and wonders, several decisions must be made at the onset of the project. Those decisions then guide the writer as he/she crafts the study. One such crucial decision is who the main audience will be. As I prayed about this question, I felt the Lord leading me to write a study for the Church. I envisioned the primary audience for this study being those who are already firmly grounded in their faith and faithfully connected to a local body of believers. That being said, it's important to note that this study is not intended to be evangelistic. This doesn't mean that the gospel is not clearly seen throughout the study; however, it *does* mean that this study is written to speak primarily to the hearts of those who are already citizens of God's eternal kingdom.

This study is also not a deep dive into all things miraculous. If you're looking for a study that will unpack every Hebrew and Greek word or wow you with fresh philosophical opinions, you'll likely be disappointed. There can be great value in studies like that. However, from the onset and throughout my work on this project, I firmly felt the hand of the Lord guiding me in the direction of simplicity.

The daily readings in this study are designed to be more of a primer than an exegetical masterpiece. In other words, my intention with the daily devotions was to find one or maybe two nuggets to pull out of the biblical text in an effort to expand the reader's understanding of miracles. Some readers will no doubt critique the lack of detail or failure to unpack some obvious points in some of these passages. But this was never my intent. The devotional readings are designed to bring the participant into consistent contact with the miraculous events contained in Scripture. These daily devotions are meant to be concise lessons that are easily absorbed, rather than long, drawn-out chapters, which is what would be needed to adequately explore all of the details of these miraculous events.

Finally, this study is not going to answer every question you have about God's signs and wonders. In fact, it might generate even more questions. While I have done my best to answer the most common questions concerning God's signs and wonders, a short study such as this one can only cover so much ground. Most of these questions are covered during the video lessons, rather than in the daily devotionals in the study. It's my prayer that by the end of this study, each participant will have a solid foundation concerning the miraculous. They will then be able to build upon that foundation long into the future.

HOW THIS STUDY IS DESIGNED

There are three main parts to this study: the daily devotions; the weekly video lesson; and the Sunday sermon. This study will produce the greatest amount of impact on the lives of those who approach it and complete it in accordance with its design.

First, each week there are five devotionals that should be read. The purpose of the devotional readings is not to teach you everything there is to know about that miracle. Rather, they are intended to expose you to a steady stream of the miraculous. Over the course of this study, you will read forty of these devotional lessons that each focus on a different miracle. Each week you will read about miracles from the Old and New Testament. Each devotional will contain encouragement, as well as something to challenge you.

To get the most out of your devotional time, it is imperative that you open your Bible and read the passage of Scripture related to the miracle in that day's study. As you read through these amazing passages of Scripture, allow the word of God to speak into your life. Next, read the devotional. Finally, finish your time with the Lord by taking a few minutes to journal in the provided space at the end of each devotion.

The second part of this study is the weekly video lesson. While the devotionals are designed to expose you to the vast array of miraculous events in the Bible, the weekly lessons are designed to dive in deeper to the major questions around God's signs and wonders. How do we identify a miracle? Do miracles still happen today? Who can perform a miracle? How many miracles are there in the Bible? These and many other questions will be explained and answered during the weekly video lessons. Following these lessons, there are a series of questions in your workbook that you should discuss with your small group.

Finally, you should make it a priority to be in church each Sunday throughout this study. Your pastor may choose to preach on the topic of signs and wonders if your church is doing this study together. However, even if your pastor is not preaching on miracles, I firmly believe that God in His sovereignty will have something special prepared for you each week. So, make the effort to be in church every Sunday while you are participating in this study.

MY PRAYER FOR YOU

My prayer for you as you begin this journey is that the Lord would open your eyes, soften your heart, and expand your perception of His glory. I pray that the Holy Spirit will guide you and overwhelm you with confidence, courage, and an outpouring of love as you awaken to the power of God in your life and the world around you. May the Lord Himself change you and challenge you as you faithfully walk with Him over the next eight weeks. Amen!

EXTRA RESOURCES

In an effort to make this small group study as affordable as possible, I have included a number of extra resources for free on my website. They include a media kit and some pastor-only resources. The media kit contains all of the small group videos, art work, PowerPoint backgrounds, countdown timers, sermon bumper videos, etc. The video teachings for each of the group lessons can also be found directly on my website.

The pastor's only material includes sermon outlines and ideas that can be utilized to develop your own messages during the course of this study. While the study can be beneficial for any group that completes it, I have found that if the entire church is engaged with the topics together, amazing things happen. I would strongly encourage you to approach this study as a church wide campaign and craft your Sunday sermons around the miracles of God. This will help everyone in your congregation be totally immersed in the signs and wonders of God over the course of eight weeks.

DOWNLOAD INSTRUCTIONS

To download these free materials, use the QR code or visit my website www.pastorpete.org. At the top of the home page, you will see a button that says "resources." You can click on this button to find all of the extra resources for this study. If you have any issues at all, please email me directly from the website using the "contact" button.

Pastor Pete

SIGNS AND WONDERS

THE MIRACLES OF GOD

WEEK ONE

WEEK ONE: LET'S GET STARTED

ICE BREAKER:

Before starting the lesson, take some time to get to know each other. Introduce yourself. As part of the introduction, answer these questions:

1. I signed up for this study because …

2. I expect to learn or experience _____ over the next eight weeks.

3. The one question I hope to get answered is?

VIDEO OUTLINE

1. Be _____

2. Be _____ of a _____

3. Be _____

4. Be _____

5. Be _____

What would you say?

☐ More Doors?

☐ More Wheels?

LET'S CONNECT

1. Website: www.pastorpete.org.
2. Facebook: @cfpastorpete
3. Twitter: @cfpastorpete
4. Instagram: pastorpetepawelek
5. Youtube: Pete Pawelek

SMALL GROUP QUESTIONS:

1. Which of the five things Pete talked about will be the hardest for you? What can you do right now to overcome those challenges?
2. What is your favorite miracle in the Bible? Why?
3. In your opinion, what is your least favorite miracle or the most confusing miracle in the Bible?
4. Will you agree to the small group covenant? Review it as a group before closing in prayer.

SMALL GROUP COVENANT

As a covenant member of my small group, I'm committed to the following qualities that honor the Lord and my fellow group members:

1. **Confidentiality:** Questions, experiences, stories, prayer requests, and anything else shared within the group will not leave the group without the permission of everyone in the group.

2. **Accountability:** I will commit to reading the devotionals and scriptures that are related to this study. I will commit to making my group a priority in my life by being on time and present for as many group meetings as possible.

3. **Engagement:** I will participate in the life of my group at a level I'm comfortable with. I will have my work completed when I arrive so that I'm prepared to be engaged in the group discussion(s).

4. **Love:** I will respect, encourage, and affirm all members of my group in a manner consistent with Christlike love.

5. **Listening:** I will listen to others with an open heart. I won't let theological differences produce division or be a distraction for me or others in my group.

6. **Prayer:** I will pray for my group and its members throughout this study.

Write other commitments your group agrees on in the space below:

_____   _____
Name   Date

WAR & WALLS

Joshua 6:20 (CSB) ... *and the wall collapsed.*

Read Joshua 6

Each time I take a group to the Holy Land, one of the places everyone is most excited to go to is Jericho. The story of the walls of this once massive and magnificent city miraculously falling to the ground is one of the first that children learn about in church. Today, Jericho is a small tourist trap of a town, but when the Israelites first crossed the Jordan, it was a major, well-fortified city dominated by trade. Archaeologists have uncovered over twenty distinct settlements of people who lived there along with the oldest fortified wall ever discovered anywhere in the world.

Jericho is literally an oasis in the middle of a desert. There are many natural springs that allow the desert to come alive in Jericho. These springs are probably the reason why humans have inhabited this site for thousands of years. For much of its history, this city sat at the crossroads of major trade and migration routes in the Jordan Valley. For this reason, the city was wealthy and thus prone to invasion and attack. Defense was not something that the inhabitants of this city had ever taken lightly.

Today, you can walk up on top of the hill, where the heart of the city once was, and look down into large archaeology pits. There, you will discover old watch towers and walls that have been uncovered. The remains of the walls that came tumbling down when Joshua and the Israelites marched on the city have also been uncovered and are available for tourists to marvel at. The might of this city and the massiveness of these walls are staggering.

However, without a single catapult, ballista, battering ram, or even a sword so much as striking the walls of Jericho, the walls fell down at the word of the Lord. If this miracle teaches us anything at all, it's that the weapons of God's warfare are very different from our own. God told Joshua before they ever set out to march around Jericho that they would be victorious in taking the well-fortified city. Israel would have literally no part in the actual battle. They would be asked simply to show up in obedience to watch the Lord work. This victory would be another gift of God's grace for His people.

The truth about walls is that everyone has them. Unlike the walls of Jericho, most of our walls are not visible to the world. They are only seen by us as we battle against them day after day. We labor and long to find a way through or a path that will lead us over the top so we can claim victory, just like the Israelites did at Jericho. However, despite our best efforts, success is elusive, and failure is far too familiar.

Perhaps the problem is not the wall but instead the weapons we choose to fight the war. What weapons are you fighting with? The carnal weapons of this world are rarely useful against the walls that stand in our way. Although God may require some of our effort in the battle, the reality is that we cannot defeat these walls on our own. There are walls in everyone's life that only God can bring down.

This doesn't mean that we sit back and do nothing at all. Joshua and the rest of the Israelites got up each day and obeyed the Lord. They did exactly what they were asked to do—no more, no less. This was the secret to their victory. It was not strategy or military might that won the battle; it was spiritual obedience that secured the victory. When we are faithful to obey, we are certain to win.

The battle and wall you are facing may be centered on an addiction. Perhaps there is a mental or emotional wall at the center of your fight. Some of the greatest walls I have seen in my life and the lives of others are in the area of failed relationships. For many, there are significant failures in their past that rise up as massive, imposing, impossible walls in their lives. Whatever your wall is composed of, know that God is greater, and His power is able to bring that wall down.

REFLECT—REFOCUS—REPENT—RESPOND

What did you hear God say today?

What will you do with what you learned?

What needs to change?

What questions do you still have?

What will you pray for?

GREAT HONOR, GREAT HATE

Acts 14:20 (CSB) — *The next day he left with Barnabas for Derbe.*

Read Acts 14:8–20

Sadly, the fickleness of humanity is one of our most distinguishable characteristics. Almost as quickly as one can change the lighting in the room with the flick of a switch, one can change their attitude about others. Initially in today's reading, we were told about the miracle of strength that was given to a man who had been lame from birth. This is the third time in the book of Acts that a crippled man had been healed. Here, we find a man who never had the strength needed to produce the power that most take for granted in our ability to walk. Paul told the man to stand up, and he did. The crowd was amazed, and immediately, they proclaimed Paul and Barnabas as gods.

Paul and Barnabas were hailed by the crowd as Zeus and Hermes. Here, we find an interesting side note: "Zeus was the chief god and Hermes the messenger equivalent to the Roman gods Jupiter and Mercury, respectively. Why, then, would Barnabas be referred to as Zeus when Paul was the leader? The answer is that Paul was the spokesman and would therefore be called Hermes and Barnabas, the more retiring of the two, would be seen as Zeus, the dignified, behind-the-scenes god."[1] Nonetheless, the two Apostles were appalled at these claims. Taking no credit for themselves, they immediately attempted to set the record straight and gave God all the glory. Even after their protesting and pleading with the crowds, the text says that *"they barely stopped the crowds from sacrificing to them."*[2] The miracle that God had performed

---

[1] Stanley D. Toussaint, "Acts," in *The Bible Knowledge Commentary: An Exposition of the Scriptures*, ed. J. F. Walvoord and R. B. Zuck, vol. 2 (Wheaton, IL: Victor Books, 1985), 392.

[2] Acts 14:18 (CSB)

through the Apostles propelled them to a place of great honor among these people. That honor, however, would soon turn into hate.

Some Jewish leaders won over the town and convinced them that Paul and Barnabas were actually evil men. We can't be certain what their claim against the Apostles was; however, it is highly likely that they brought the accusation of blasphemy against them since the punishment for blasphemy was death by stoning. Whatever the charge, this was the second of five separate incidents in which violence was used against Paul by the Jews.

We are not told why the punishment was only carried out on Paul. It was not mentioned that Barnabas was stoned or punished, and our curiosity concerning his whereabouts during this event can't be satisfied by the biblical record. We are told, however, that Paul was severely stoned to the point that the crowd believed he was dead. They dragged him out of the city and left his fatally wounded body there. The local disciples, presumably including Barnabas, later gathered around his body. What happened next was miraculous. Paul got up and decided to walk back into the city and stay the night.

Once again, many details are missing from the narrative. Some believe that Paul was actually killed and then brought back to life so his ministry could continue. Others believe he was only stunned and knocked out and eventually regained consciousness. We are also left to wonder what happened that night. When Paul walked back into town, it is not a stretch to assume that people noticed. After the events of the day and all that had led to his conviction and stoning, it is unlikely that he was able to blend in very well walking through the town square. The text does not indicate that Paul or his companions made any attempt to hide his identity or conceal him. I suspect that the spectators at this point, having seen Paul and Barnabas heal the lame man and having watched a dead man walking back into town, probably thought, Maybe we should leave that guy alone! Whatever the case, a miracle of healing happened not only in the life of the lame man but in the physical restoration of

Paul's body as well. After being stoned to the point people thought he was dead, he was able to get up and walk back into the city under his own power.

The very next day, Paul and Barnabas wisely left for Derbe. Here again, we see the wonder-working power of God's restoration. There is no mention of soreness, lingering wounds, or Paul needing to be transported by other means while his body healed from the turmoil of the previous day's beating. He walked back into town, and now he walked out of town. Later, Paul would recount his trial in Lystra to Timothy. In 2 Timothy 3:10–11 Paul writes, *"But you have followed my teaching, conduct, purpose, faith, patience, love, and endurance, along with the persecutions and sufferings that came to me in Antioch, Iconium, and Lystra. What persecutions I endured—and yet the Lord rescued me from them all."*

Whatever trial, temptations, tragedy, or persecution you may face in life, never forget that God has the power to rescue you from them all!

REFLECT—REFOCUS—REPENT—RESPOND

What did you hear God say today?

What will you do with what you learned?

What needs to change?

What questions do you still have?

What will you pray for?

DISCRETE INTENTIONS

Numbers 22:22 (CSB) —*But God was incensed that Balaam was going ...*

Read Numbers 22:1–41

I don't know of anyone who can honestly say they haven't at one time or another attempted to fool God. For one reason or another, everyone has tried to pull something over on God at some point in their life. This was exactly what happened here in Numbers 22, where we find the miracle of the talking donkey. Unfortunately, more people know about the talking donkey in the movie *Shrek* than they do about this miracle in Numbers 22.

Some compounding miracles took place in this chapter of Scripture. First, we must deal with the fact that God chose to speak to Balaam at all because Balaam was a "seer" not a seeker or follower of God in any way. Many have correctly inferred that his profession was to practice in what we might call the *"occult"* today. He was someone who was known to have a connection to the supernatural realm and was so respected that kings such as Balak, in this case, would hire him to help them summon supernatural power when it was needed. Here, Balak was willing to pay Balaam to curse God's people.

Balaam's response when the messengers arrived is interesting. He said to the king's messengers, *"Spend the night here, and I will give you the answer the* **Lord** *tells me."*[3] The word used for *"Lord"* here is YHWH, signifying that Balaam's intention from the start was to connect with God himself. While this may not make any sense to us, it made perfect sense to Balaam. Pagan prophets such as Balaam believed that people's own personal gods had the greatest power over them. This is why Balaam

---

[3] Numbers 22:8 (CSB)

wanted to establish some kind of connection with the God of the Israelites.

God indeed responded to this soothsayer and told him explicitly not to go back with the king's messengers and not to curse the Israelites. God told Balaam that His people were blessed. Balaam then told the kings' messengers he could not do as they had requested or return with them because YHWH would not permit it. The messengers were sent back a second time after returning to the king with the news of Balaam's refusal. This time, they had enhanced the reward for the pagan prophet's curse upon God's people. After consulting with the Lord again, Balaam was given permission to go with them but strictly ordered that he must only do what God said.

Balaam left the very next morning in what looked like full obedience to God. However, this is where we see the discrete intentions of Balaam surface. After gaining God's permission, Numbers 22:22 says that *"God was incensed that Balaam was going."* On the surface, this makes God look double-minded. However, the reality is that Balaam departed with his own personal agenda on the top of his mind. This might have been the money he was expecting to receive or perhaps the power, fame, and notoriety that he felt was going to be his following this mission. Whatever it was, God could see his real intentions and was not fooled.

As Balaam was on his way to meeting with Balak, we see the most obvious miracle in this passage. God chose to give the donkey both divine vision and voice. First, the donkey was able to see what this pagan prophet could not. After the donkey endured three beatings at the hand of Balaam, God allowed the donkey to speak and confront Balaam for his abuse. The Lord opened the donkey's mouth and she actually said to Balaam, *"What have I done to you that you have beaten me these three times?"*[4] Stranger still is the fact that Balaam did not seem alarmed by the donkey's question. Instead, Balaam simply answered the donkey's question, and

---

[4] Numbers 22:28 (CSB)

then the donkey talked again! Only then did God perform another miraculous thing by allowing Balaam himself the vision needed to see the angel of the Lord in the path, with his sword in hand.

It is here that we find that a genuine transformation and sincere willingness to obey God has developed inside Balaam. He even offered to turn around and go home, but the angel said, *"Go with the men, but you are to say only what I tell you. So Balaam went with Balak's officials."*[5] Now God had his full attention. When Balaam arrived before the king, he started by announcing *"Look, I have come to you, but can I say anything I want? I must speak only the message God puts in my mouth."*[6]

Some find it hard to believe that God would speak to a pagan prophet, much less use him for divine purposes. Others find it impossible to believe that a donkey could speak or have the vision to see an angel. I suppose the same people might find it hard to believe that the blind regained their sight, the deaf their hearing, and the mute their voices. I find it no harder to believe a donkey can talk than to believe that Jesus walked out of the grave on the third day. There is nothing impossible for our God! The miracle itself is never the message; instead, the message is always *inside* the miracle. Here, we are reminded that our obedience to the Lord is of the utmost importance and that our discrete intentions are never hidden from God.

---

[5] Numbers 22:35 (CSB)

[6] Numbers 22:38 (CSB)

REFLECT—REFOCUS—REPENT—RESPOND

What did you hear God say today?

What will you do with what you learned?

What needs to change?

What questions do you still have?

What will you pray for?

SIMPLY COMPASSION

Matthew 15:32 (CSB) — *I have compassion on the crowd...*

Read Matthew 15:29–39

The feeding of the four thousand parallels another miracle commonly known as the feeding of the five thousand (Matthew 14:13–21). Both of these feeding miracles display numerous lessons for those who received the miracles from Christ and for those who reflect on them still today. The exact number of those fed on these occasions is not known, but it is most certainly many more than nine thousand people in total. While many of us struggle to prepare a meal for the handful of occupants in our own home, Jesus fed the multitudes without ever breaking a sweat.

Many suggest that these two miracles are one in the same. Some modern theologians suggest that due to their immense similarities, along with their close proximity in the gospel accounts, the feeding miracles must be duplicated accounts of the same event. However, on closer examination, it is clear that Jesus actually just performed a similar miracle on two different occasions. Just as he healed more than one leper, gave sight to more than one blind man, and cast demons out of people multiple times, it is not difficult to imagine that He could feed thousands of people multiple times as well.

According to Scripture, the motives for the miracles in both instances are different. It has been noted that the feeding of the five thousand was likely for a largely Jewish audience, whereas the feeding of the four thousand may have included mostly Gentiles. This speculation came about because the miracles clearly happened in two different locations. The five thousand were fed at the northern end of the Sea of Galilee near Bethsaida the hometown of the apostles Peter, Andrew, and Phillip (John 1:44). However, the four thousand were fed on the eastern shore of the lake in the region of the Decapolis, where Gentiles were the majority. In the accounts of the feeding of the five thousand, Jesus had just crossed the lake but was pursued by large crowds. After the feeding miracle of the five thousand, Jesus sent the disciples away by boat. That was when a fierce storm arose, and Jesus walked on the water. With the feeding of the four thousand, Jesus was coming from the region of Tyre and Sidon, and there is no mention of a storm or walking on the water. It is hard to imagine that someone would have left that out of the narrative, which points again to two separate miraculous feeding miracles.

There are a few other differences that are harder to see. For example, in the feeding of the five thousand, Jesus was only with the people for a day, but here, He had been with them for three days. The five thousand were fed with five loaves and two fish. Here, during the feeding of the four thousand, despite there being a smaller number of people present for the occasion, seven loaves and a few small fish are mentioned. Perhaps most telling are the different words used for *basket* in the accounts. In the feeding of the five thousand, the Greek word *kophinos* is used. These were small wicker baskets that held one or two gallons of provisions. However, in the feeding of the four thousand, the word *spyris* is used. This is specifically a much larger basket, as noted in the text in Matthew 15. It can mean a hamper and would later describe the kind of basket that was used to lower Paul down through the opening in the city wall in Acts 9. Thus, two different words were used to describe two very different-sized baskets. Twelve small baskets were used to collect all of the leftovers in the feeding of the five thousand, while only seven of the much larger baskets were used here. When you look closely, it is easy to see that these are two separate miraculous events.

Perhaps the most important thing about this miracle, however, is Christ's motivation to perform it. Here, we find no challenge from the Pharisees. There is no emergency or life-threatening situation developing. Here, Jesus did not need to offer any proof of His divine abilities or nature to satisfy the crowds. There was no clear necessity for this miracle to advance His divine mission in any way. Instead, at the heart of this miracle, we simply find the compassion of Christ. He cared about these faithful men and women who had been with Him now for three days, and he did not want to send them away hungry. How sweet it is to know that we have a savior who cares for not only our spiritual needs but also our physical needs from the depths of His divine compassion.

SIGNS AND WONDERS

REFLECT—REFOCUS—REPENT—RESPOND

What did you hear God say today?

What will you do with what you learned?

What needs to change?

What questions do you still have?

What will you pray for?

A MIRACLE OF GRACE

Jonah 3:4 (CSB) — *"In forty days Nineveh will be demolished!"*

Read Jonah Chapters 3 & 4

Charles Reade sums up the book of Jonah well in saying: "The book of Jonah is the most beautiful story ever written in so small a compass." It's a shame that today this tiny treasure is largely overlooked and underappreciated, except for the part about Jonah living inside the belly of the whale for three days. While that is a miracle too, in my opinion it's not the greatest miracle recorded in this book.

Jonah's story is a roller coaster ride. Jonah was at one time a faithful prophet and had previously been used by the Lord. 2 Kings 14:25 is the first mention of Jonah in Scripture: *"He restored Israel's border from Lebo-hamath as far as the Sea of the Arabah, according to the word the Lord, the God of Israel, had spoken through his servant, the prophet Jonah son of Amittai from Gath-hepher."* Despite his past faithfulness to the Lord, the book that bears his name chronicles his resistance to God's will. Here, we find the Lord's patience on full display as God brings Jonah safely, miraculously, and mercifully to a place where he must obey.

Most consider the climax of this story to be the sparing of Jonah's life as he was tossed into the sea by the sailors aboard his ship in an effort to save their own lives. As he entered the sea in the middle of a terrible storm, his fate seemed certain. He would soon meet God in eternity and give and account for his rebellion and resistance. But instead, God had put a fish there in the water beneath the waves that would swallow this man whole and entomb him for three days. Then, just as clearly as God had spoken to Jonah (in Jonah 2:10), God spoke to the fish. His command was simple and immediately obeyed by the sea creature. He vomited the now-repentant prophet up on the beach.

Jonah then received another opportunity to exercise obedience and become a vessel for God and help bring about the greatest miracle in this story. In Jonah 3:1–2 (CSB) it says, *"The word of the Lord came to Jonah a second time: Get up! Go to the great city of Nineveh and preach the message that I tell you."* This time, Jonah got up and reluctantly went. Upon his arrival in Nineveh, he took a walk and preached the shortest message of revival ever recorded. In my translation, there are only seven simple words proclaimed by the reluctant prophet: *"In forty days, Nineveh will be demolished!"* He did not learn to preach like that in seminary, I can assure you. But from this simple, short and straightforward warning, we see the miracle of God's grace sweep across the city. Indeed, it is the miracle that most miss: the miracle of sackcloth found in verse five, when the people of this wicked city repented and believed in God.

This was not an isolated miracle. The text says that everyone in the city, from the greatest to the lowest, believed in God. The king himself departed his personal throne, removed his royal robe, repented, and sat in the sackcloth. How precious it must have been to the heart of the Lord to see the king, who was the most powerful person in the entire empire, take this low and humble position. Sackcloth is a coarsely woven garment normally made from goat hair. It was something that was put on in times of mourning and seasons of grief in ancient times. It was also a sign of submission and self-humiliation to wear sackcloth and sit in ashes.

More than anything else, we see the miracle of grace throughout this short book. God is gracious to the crude sailors, to the wayward prophet, and to the people of this wicked city. We can be certain that the miracle of grace is still available today. You might relate your life to that of the ignorant sailors, the reluctant and rebellious prophet, or the people of the wicked and wretched city of Nineveh. Nonetheless, the grace of God is available to you and everyone you know as well. His name is Jesus, and His work was finished on the cross of Calvary. Your sins have been forgiven, and His grace is here.

If this entire city could experience the miracle of grace by hearing seven simple words from a rebellious prophet, surely you can hear it in three words from the Lamb of God. They were His last words, and they are precious words of grace: *"It is FINISHED!"* God loves you, Jesus died for you, and His Spirit is alive inside of you. Rise from the ashes and rejoice in the miracle of grace.

REFLECT—REFOCUS—REPENT—RESPOND

What did you hear God say today?

What will you do with what you learned?

What needs to change?

What questions do you still have?

What will you pray for?

SIGNS AND WONDERS

THE MIRACLES OF GOD

WEEK TWO

WEEK TWO: BIBLICAL IDENTIFICATION

ICE BREAKER:

Prior to the group arriving, the group leader should find six to ten common household items and place them in a box or bowl to conceal the identity of the items from the other group members as they arrive.

Before you start the video, select two group members to be blindfolded. Divide the items in half. One by one, hand each of the blindfolded members a household item and see if they can identify them correctly. Keep score if you like.

Finally, after all of the items have been identified, have the spouse of the blindfolded person and one or two other members of the group who are the same sex as the spouse say one by one, "Our group is awesome" and see if each of the blindfolded individuals can identify their spouse. For bonus points see if they can identify other members of the group when they hear their voice.

Tips:

1. It's best to have one male and one female be the blindfolded participant. They should not be married to each other.

2. Don't use sharp or otherwise dangerous items. You don't want someone to cut themselves or otherwise harm themselves as they handle the items.

3. Try to select common household items but not things that are super easy to identify. For example, a "fork" is probably not the best choice to make the game fun.

SIGNS AND WONDERS

VIDEO OUTLINE

I. How does the Bible _____ to the miraculous?

    A. _____ and _____

    B. _____

        1. **Exodus 3:20 (CSB)** —²⁰ *But when I stretch out my hand and strike Egypt with all my miracles that I will perform in it, after that, he will let you go.*

        2. **Psalm 118:23 (CSB)** —²³ *This came from the Lord; it is wondrous in our sight.*

        3. **Exodus 7:8–9 (CSB)** —⁸ *The Lord said to Moses and Aaron,⁹ "When Pharaoh tells you, 'Perform a miracle,' tell Aaron, 'Take your staff and throw it down before Pharaoh. It will become a serpent.'"*

        4. **Daniel 4:2–3 (CSB)** —² *I am pleased to tell you about the miracles and wonders the Most High God has done for me.³ How great are his miracles, and how mighty his* **wonders***! His kingdom is an eternal kingdom, and his dominion is from generation to generation.*

    C. _____

        1. **Mark 5:30 (CSB)** —³⁰ *Immediately Jesus realized that power had gone out from him. He turned around in the crowd and said, "Who touched my clothes?"*

        2. **Luke 6:18–19 (CSB)** —¹⁸ *They came to hear him and to be healed of their diseases; and those tormented by unclean spirits were made well.¹⁹ The whole crowd was trying to touch him, because power was coming out from him and healing them all.*

3. **Acts 19:11 (CSB)** —*¹¹ God was performing extraordinary miracles by Paul's hands.*

4. **Acts 19:11 (NLT)** —*¹¹ God gave Paul the power to perform unusual miracles.*

5. **Mark 6:5 (CSB)** —*⁵ He was not able to do a miracle there, except that he laid his hands on a few sick people and healed them.*

D. Mighty _____

1. **Matthew 11:20 (ESV)** —*²⁰ Then he began to denounce the cities where most of his mighty works had been done, because they did not repent.*

2. **Matthew 13:54 (ESV)** —*⁵⁴… and coming to his hometown he taught them in their synagogue, so that they were astonished, and said, "Where did this man get this wisdom and these mighty works?"*

3. **Deuteronomy 11:2–3 (CSB)** —*² Understand today that it is not your children who experienced or saw the discipline of the Lord your God: His greatness, strong hand, and outstretched arm;³ his signs and the works he did in Egypt to Pharaoh king of Egypt and all his land.*

4. **1 Chronicles 16:9–12 (CSB)** —*⁹ Sing to him; sing praise to him; tell about all his wondrous works!¹⁰ Boast in his holy name; let the hearts of those who seek the Lord rejoice.¹¹ Seek the Lord and his strength; seek his face always.¹² Remember the wondrous works he has done, his wonders, and the judgments he has pronounced.*

SIGNS AND WONDERS

E. _____ Things

1. **Luke 5:25–26 (CSB)** —*²⁵Immediately he got up before them, picked up what he had been lying on, and went home glorifying God. ²⁶Then everyone was astounded, and they were giving glory to God. And they were filled with awe and said, "We have seen incredible things today."*

    i. "Para" meaning "_____"

    ii. "Doxa" meaning "_____"

"_____" point to the theological meaning of miracle as a revelation of God, "_____" to the force behind the act, "_____" to the person behind it, and "_____" to its "awesome" effect on the observer.[7]

---

[7] Walter A. Elwell and Barry J. Beitzel, "Miracle," *Baker Encyclopedia of the Bible* (Grand Rapids, MI: Baker Book House, 1988), 1468–1469.

SMALL GROUP QUESTIONS:

1. Why do you think different translations use different English words or phrases to describe the same things in Scripture?

2. What other ways have you seen the biblical text describe or identify God's signs and wonders?

3. How would you summarize the meaning behind each of the main words we discussed today?

    a. Signs and Wonders

    b. Miracles

    c. Power

    d. Works

    e. Incredible Things

4. If you could only use one of these terms, we discussed today to describe God's signs and wonders, which would you choose? Why?

5. In general, do you think people are comfortable talking about the miracles of God? Why or why not?

6. Thinking back on this week's devotional readings, which one surprised you the most? Which did you find the most interesting? Take some time to discuss your questions or thoughts about the devotional readings with each other as you finish up your group time.

MASS MIRACLES

Luke 4:40 (CSB) — *When the sun was setting, all those who had anyone sick with various diseases brought them to him. As he laid his hands on each one of them, he healed them.*

Read Matthew 8:1–17

Relatively few of the miracles Christ performed were for large masses of people. Generally, the narratives revolve around a single blind man, perhaps a few with leprosy, or a needy woman. While not unique, the account of the mass healings in Capernaum is not the way Christ normally operated when it came to miracles.

It was late in the day before the mass miracle event started because this took place on the Sabbath. Barclay notes that "According to the Sabbath law, which forbade all work on the Sabbath day, it was illegal to heal on the Sabbath. Steps could be taken to prevent a person from getting any worse, but no steps might be taken to make that person any better. The general law was that on the Sabbath medical attention might only be given to those whose lives were actually in danger. Further, it was illegal to carry a burden on the Sabbath day, and a burden was anything which weighed more than two dried figs. It was, therefore, illegal to carry a sick person from place to place on a stretcher or in one's arms or on one's shoulders, for to do so would have been to carry a burden."[8] Officially, the Sabbath did not end until two stars could clearly be seen in the night sky. This is why the crowd waited to bring their sick so late in the day.

Before we consider that Jesus worked late into the night to bring relief to all of those in desperate need of His generosity of grace, we must

---

[8] William Barclay, *The Gospel of Matthew*, Rev. and updated., *The New Daily Study Bible* (Edinburgh: Saint Andrew Press, 2001), 357–358.

remember that he had been busy this entire Sabbath day. Jesus had almost certainly taught early in the day at the synagogue. He had also healed a demon-possessed man and healed the centurion's servant. When He arrived at Peter's home, he learned that Peter's mother was sick, so He cured her of her fever. In fact, she was so fully healed that she started to serve Him immediately following the healing. No doubt Jesus had also had to deal with those who were jealous of His ministry and looking for any reason to accuse and arrest Him. It's fair to say that this had been a full day before the masses ever showed up.

Although Jesus had the power, ability, and divine authority to simply say the word or wave His hand and heal everyone who was waiting in line, this was not what he did. Luke tells us that "*He laid his hands on each one of them.*"[9] Christ's love and compassion were such that He did not hurry through His work. Instead, He gave each person and each family the love they deserved. Although everyone who witnessed the events of this day saw a miracle, it is likely that many missed the miracle Jesus Himself was as the Messiah.

The manifestation of His power on this day was miraculous. It brings the curious mind to wonder even more about how much unused power was still available when the final miracle was completed. Indeed, the wonder-working power of Christ is limitless and will never run dry, so long as there is a soul in need of His touch. How precious the touch of Christ must have been to those in Capernaum on this historic day, when so many were set free. Indeed, how precious is the touch of Christ today for those who will seek the favor of His limitless grace in their own situations.

---

[9] Luke 4:40 CSB

REFLECT—REFOCUS—REPENT—RESPOND

What did you hear God say today?

What will you do with what you learned?

What needs to change?

What questions do you still have?

What will you pray for?

MANNA

Exodus 16:4 (CSB) — *Then the Lord said to Moses, "I am going to rain bread from heaven for you."*

Read Exodus 16:1–35

There is a substantial difference between complaining *to* God and complaining *about* God. Here we find God's chosen people doing the latter. According to verse seven in this chapter, despite all of the miracles they had witnessed thus far in their exodus, their mistrust and ingratitude toward God was put on full display, and they complained *about* Him. Oh, how they longed for the pots of meat that were previously theirs during their captivity in Egypt. This was not the first time, nor would it be the last time they would express their displeasure in their heavenly Father.

In response to their complaints about Him, God announced through Moses that He would provide for His people. The Israelites would eventually name the substance *manna*. To this day, no-one knows exactly what manna was. However, we do know many important things about this mysterious food that fell from Heaven six mornings a week. For example, we know that it was miraculously rationed by God. You could only take what you needed, and that which was not used would rot before the next day. When it came to manna, everyone in camp was on equal footing. Exodus 16:18 says, *"When they measured it by quarts, the person who gathered a lot had no surplus, and the person who gathered a little had no shortage. Each gathered as much as he needed to eat."* God miraculously ensured that everyone had just enough.

We know from Numbers 19 that the manna arrived each day with the morning dew. We know that it had the taste of honey wafers and satisfied the nutritional needs of God's people. We know that the only labor required to receive this divine provision was the minimal effort to gather it from the ground. A double portion was supplied on the sixth day, and none could be found on the seventh day of each week. This miraculous, perfectly portioned gift from God was supplied for no fewer than forty years as God's people wandered in the wilderness. Finally, we know that God's people grew to loathe this miraculous gift (Num 21:5).

How strange it is to consider the prospect of despising such a miraculous gift. Some argue that if anyone eats the same thing for forty years, they will grow to hate it. The Israelites, however, did not only eat manna. While it was a dependable and important part of their diet, it was hardly all they had to eat. They had various kinds of livestock on their journey that they ate and sacrificed. In the book of Numbers, we learn that they possessed flour. In Deuteronomy 2:6, God's people are instructed that trading and purchasing food from the inhabitants of the land they would pass through were permissible. No doubt, as they wandered in the wilderness, God's people also consumed wildlife, berries, plants, fish, and other things. To believe that all they ate for forty years was manna is false. And yet, they still came to detest it.

We might be tempted to think too highly of ourselves and say, "*I would never despise God's miraculous work in my life!*" The Devil and his demons love to blind us in this way. I'm certain that those on the Exodus journey failed to realize how foolish it was to hate God's miraculous gift, just as most Christians do today. On the first day of the miraculous manifestation of God's grace in our lives through salvation in Jesus Christ, we loved it. However, over the years and decades, most come to loathe it. After some time has passed, we grow comfortable with the steady provision of grace that comes with following Christ. As we mature, we begin to realize that we are a part of a greater kingdom, of which Christ is the king. Although we celebrate His kingship and are grateful to be a part of the kingdom, we despise the rules of the kingdom and the commands of the king. Thus, we do not give generously according to His standard. We fail to gather with others each week and to be faithful members of the Body of Christ. We live our lives, plan our weekends, budget our money, and otherwise just go about doing everything the way we want to. It's not because we haven't experienced the miraculous grace of God. The truth is that we have come to loathe the reality of having a king and not being the king or queen of our own kingdom.

Be thankful for the manna …

SIGNS AND WONDERS

REFLECT—REFOCUS—REPENT—RESPOND

What did you hear God say today?

What will you do with what you learned?

What needs to change?

What questions do you still have?

What will you pray for?

HEALING & HATRED

John 5:8 (CSB) — *"Get up," Jesus told him, "pick up your mat and walk."*

Read John 5:1–23

The crippled man in this passage had received a miracle on the grandest scale. His incurable condition was instantly cured at the word of Christ. One might think this would be a reason for universal joy among anyone who ran into the man walking down the street. However, the orthodox Jews who saw the man took the opportunity to remind him that it was against the Sabbath law to carry his mat down the street. As is so frequently the case with the miracles of Jesus, this healing intensified the hatred His enemies had for Him.

Jesus performed no fewer than seven miraculous healings on the Sabbath throughout His ministry. These healings were among the most despised by the religious leaders. It is hard for most to understand how important the Sabbath is to practicing Jews. Still to this day, orthodox Jews follow the law of the Sabbath to extremes most people in Western civilization can scarcely comprehend. For instance, when traveling through the international airport in Israel on the Sabbath, you will notice that the majority of the restaurants and shops are closed. Why? Because it is the Sabbath, so any business owned by a practicing Jew will not be open. Once on a trip to the Holy Land, our group was staying at a large hotel owned by a Jewish family. On Saturday, when our group and hundreds of other tourists showed up for breakfast, we found that the dining hall was empty and that there were boiled eggs and loaves of bread next to a row of toasters. When someone from our group approached the front desk to voice their complaints, they found the front desk abandoned. There was no room service that day, either. I must admit it was slightly humorous watching all of the American tourists trying to wrap their minds around this event. So serious is the command to Sabbath that orthodox Jews abandon international airports and hotels

SIGNS AND WONDERS

each week for an entire day. The Sabbath is no trivial matter, and in the time of Christ, it was even more intense.

The crippled man had been sitting in the same place for a long time. The healing waters of this pool were known around the world. "Beneath the pool was a subterranean stream which every now and again bubbled up and disturbed the waters. The belief was that the disturbance was caused by an angel, and that the first person to get into the pool after the troubling of the water would be healed from any illness from which he or she was suffering."[10] Because this man was crippled and had no-one to help him, his miracle had been stolen from him time and time again. But not this day. For the Son of God simply said, *"Get up!"* Always a friend to the friendless and a helper to the helpless, Jesus provided for this man's greatest need.

Outraged and unimpressed by the power of Christ, the haters attempted to extract an explanation from Jesus. His response was simple and succinct, *"My Father is still working, and I am working also."*[11] To this, the biblical record reports the following in John 5:17: *"This is why the Jews began trying all the more to kill him."* The verbs used in John 5:17 are in the imperfect tense, which is used to describe repeated action in the past. It is clear that this was not the only offense Jesus had committed on the Sabbath in the eyes of the Jewish leaders. This, however, does not change the point Jesus was trying to illustrate: namely, that the compassion and love of God never rests, even on the Sabbath.

Over the years many have attempted to explain Jesus' point in different ways. "Philo said: 'God never ceases doing, but as it is the property of fire to burn and snow to chill, so it is the property of God to do.' Another writer said: 'The sun shines; the rivers flow; the processes

---

[10] William Barclay, *The Gospel of John*, Rev. and updated., vol. 1, *The New Daily Study Bible* (Edinburgh: Saint Andrew Press, 2001), 207.

[11] John 5:17 CSB

of birth and death go on the Sabbath as on any other day; and that is the work of God.' True, according to the creation story, God rested on the seventh day; but he rested from creation; his higher works of judgment and mercy and compassion and love still went on."[12] The healing Christ performed on this day was justified; the hatred he received was not.

From this miracle, we learn that it is wise to rest from the physical and mental demands of life. These are never attacked or challenged by Christ. However, the spiritual work of compassion, grace, love, peace, generosity, and service should never be neglected. These and others like them are the holy work of God, which should be a constant force in the life of a disciple.

---

[12] William Barclay, <u>The Gospel of John</u>, Rev. and updated., vol. 1, *The New Daily Study Bible* (Edinburgh: Saint Andrew Press, 2001), 213.

SIGNS AND WONDERS

REFLECT—REFOCUS—REPENT—RESPOND

What did you hear God say today?

What will you do with what you learned?

What needs to change?

What questions do you still have?

What will you pray for?

DRY BONES

2 Kings 13:21 (CSB) —*When he touched Elisha's bones, the man revived and stood up.*

Read 2 Kings 13:14–21

The prophet Elisha was the son of Shaphat from Abel-meholah (1 Kings 19:16). Elisha was called in ministry by Elijah during Ahab's reign, which ended in 853 B.C. We are told that Elisha died in Jehoash's reign, which began in 798 B.C. So we know that this man's ministry spanned a minimum of fifty-six years. However, many biblical scholars believe his ministry lasted closer to sixty years, which is amazing. During that time, this man of God labored for the Lord on behalf of the nation of Israel. He had a profound concern for God's chosen people. No fewer than sixteen miracles are attributed to his ministry, doubling the eight attributed to his mentor Elijah.

Perhaps the most powerful and interesting miracle of all related to Elijah is this one, which occurred following his death. I have to wonder if, after watching his mentor Elijah whisked away into Heaven without experiencing death, Elisha thought his own journey into eternity might happen in a similar manner. However, his fate was like that of most of us. He grew older and older with each passing year. His body broke down, and the days of vigor and health afforded to him in his youth disappeared. He became ill, and when his time was done, he died. His legacy and ministry, however, would continue for years to come. This is something we can all take comfort in knowing: that even when our time on earth is over, God has the power to continue to use our lives to bless and influence the lives of those who remain.

Like most Old Testament prophets, the miraculous events that happened through Elisha's ministry took place during his lifetime. God chose, on fifteen occasions, to manifest His power in miraculous ways through Elisha's life. What makes him stand out from the rest is that even after Elisha's death, we see God use his bones to provide life to a man who was dead. It is this sixteenth miracle of Elisha that so clearly shows us all how insignificant we are in the workings of God, for we see that the power to perform the miraculous does not find its source in us at all but solely in the will of God. We also see that God's purposes are not always clearly visible, even when it comes to His signs and wonders.

We are not told how long Elisha had been in the grave when this event occurred. It can take months or even several years for a human body to fully decompose, depending on environmental conditions. Due to Elisha's prominence in the kingdom, it is most likely that he was laid to rest in a tomb. The custom was to lay the body out and allow it to decay over time in the tomb. It was not unusual for multiple people to occupy a single tomb in ancient times. After decomposition, their bones would normally be placed in a box to preserve space and make room for new bodies. It appears that enough time had passed for Elisha's physical body to decompose, but no-one had yet collected his bones and moved them into the ossuary.

The miracle occurred when some men in the process of burying another man were startled to hear or see Moabite raiders approaching fast. They hastily tossed this unknown man onto the bones of Elisha to make a quick escape and save their own lives. To their amazement, the dead man they had planned to seal in the tomb that day jumped up and was now alive again. Sadly, that's where the story ends. We are not told what happened to the man, and we are left to wonder what God's purpose for this miracle might have been.

Perhaps God's purpose is not found in relation to this man who was brought back to life but instead in relation to the nation of Israel. Following the death of Elisha, the nation of Israel hit hard times. They were oppressed, attacked, and discouraged time and time again. During his lifetime, Elisha was the prophet who spoke for God. However, the massive number of miracles performed through his ministry also proved how faithful, mighty, and merciful God was. The miracle of raising the dead man with Elisha's dry bones seems to be a reminder of those things that God sent to the nation of Israel sometime after Elisha's death. It is as if God was saying, "My promises still stand, my power is still valid, and my mercy is still available. If I can do this from dry bones, imagine what I could do through you!"

There is little doubt that the news of this event spread quickly throughout Israel and the surrounding countries. This was the first and last miracle produced from the bones of a dead man. But it is just one miracle among many that points to the marvelous and merciful nature of our God. This is why we never celebrate the miracle; rather, we celebrate the God of miracles.

REFLECT—REFOCUS—REPENT—RESPOND

What did you hear God say today?

What will you do with what you learned?

What needs to change?

What questions do you still have?

What will you pray for?

NO ANSWERS

Luke 14:6 (CSB) —*They could find no answer to these things.*

Read Luke 14:1–24

Jesus was well known as a miracle worker at this point in His ministry. This would be His seventh and final Sabbath miracle. Almost from the beginning, the religious leaders had opposed Jesus, particularly on issues of the Sabbath. As was often the case, the Pharisees enjoyed the sport of ambush. It was the custom of the Pharisees to share a simple meal following a synagogue on the Sabbath. The invitation Christ received to this Sabbath meal, however, was not one of sincerity but rather one of deception and false motives.

The Pharisees attempted to trap Jesus once again. While we can't be certain, it appears that the Pharisees planted a seriously ill man in a room in an effort to trick Jesus. This man had what was referred to as dropsy, or what is known today as edema. This is a particularly dangerous and debilitating condition. This man was suffering from the accumulation of watery fluid in his tissue, likely caused by another disorder with his heart, kidneys, or liver. He was not only sick but was almost certainly being used as a pawn in the Pharisees' ambush of Jesus. This sick man had likely never been invited to this dinner before. The Pharisees did not care about this man or his healing. He was nothing more than the bait for the trap. It is easy to imagine how much shame and embarrassment this man would have felt, sitting in the middle of this crowd made up with the exception of Jesus of elite and self-entitled religious leaders.

Jesus knew the hearts of each and every person in the room that day. Thus, Jesus took the initiative to intervene in the situation. First, He asked if it was lawful for Him to perform a miracle and heal this man on the Sabbath. No-one said a word; the room was still and quiet as Jesus took the bait. In my mind, I see the sick man looking at the floor in

SIGNS AND WONDERS

disgrace and discomfort, knowing that he was the sick man being singled out by this question. Then slowly raising his eyes from the floor, he made eye contact with the loving eyes of Jesus. Jesus then took this man, healed him, and according to the text, sent him away from this den of humiliation. The sick man was now whole, his life was forever changed, his body was fully healed, and his torment was transformed into a testimony he would share with others for the rest of his life.

The primary lesson in this passage focuses on the Sabbath and what should or should not be done on the Sabbath. However, there is another lesson here in the middle of the miracle. This message is one we must not miss. You see, it's entirely possible to watch Jesus closely and fail to see who he really is. You would think that everyone in the room that day would have hit their knees, repented of their sins, and become followers of Christ. However, that was not the case. Despite seeing this miracle with their own eyes and facing two simple questions raised by Christ, they still could not find answers to these things. Even today, there are many who have seen, heard, and watched the work of Christ closely for a long time and are yet to repent of their sins and call on Jesus as Lord.

When confronted with the miraculous, the Pharisees' hatred for Jesus and their rejection of His ministry only intensified. No-one was watching Jesus more closely than they were, and despite numerous signs and wonders pointing to the Messiahship of Christ, the Pharisees failed to make the connection. One of the great tragedies of the modern Church is very similar. Namely, there are countless people who are watching closely yet are still far from faithful.

My prayer is that if this describes you, you will not continue down this road of the Pharisees. Instead, I pray that you would at this very moment ask the Lord for forgiveness and place your trust in Him. In so doing, you'll find yourself the recipient of the miracle of salvation and grace that can only be found in Jesus Christ. When it comes to any miracle you see or hear about, the answer is always Jesus! It's sad to know that these Pharisees who watched Jesus so closely missed the Messiah when He performed a miracle at their own table.

REFLECT—REFOCUS—REPENT—RESPOND

What did you hear God say today?

What will you do with what you learned?

What needs to change?

What questions do you still have?

What will you pray for?

SIGNS AND WONDERS

THE MIRACLES OF GOD

WEEK THREE

WEEK THREE: LET'S GET REAL

ICE BREAKER:

Take some time before today's video lesson to share about a time in your childhood when your expectations ran into reality. Think about a time from your childhood or adolescence when your wide-eyed expectations, goals, or dreams outpaced reality. Take time to let everyone in the group share about a totally unrealistic dream or expectation they had as a child.

VIDEO OUTLINE

I. How many _____ are in the Bible?

   A. I think there are _____ miracles in the Bible.

      1. There are _____ chapters in the Bible.

      2. There are _____ verses in the Bible.

      3. And the Bible covers approximately _____ years of history.

II. _____

   A. "An _____ event manifesting divine intervention in human affairs" (*Merriam Webster Dictionary*).

SIGNS AND WONDERS

    B. "An event that defies common expectations of behavior and subsequently is attributed to a _____ agent; an occurrence that demonstrates God's involvement in the course of human affairs" (*The Lexham Bible Dictionary*).

    C. "Events which unmistakably involve an _____ and _____ action of God designed to reveal His character or purposes" (*Holman Illustrated Bible Dictionary*).

    D. "Events which may seem contrary to nature and which signifies an act in which God _____ himself to man" (*Baker Encyclopedia of the Bible*).

    E. "A work wrought by a divine _____, for a divine _____ by means beyond the reach of man" (*Herbert Lockyer*).

    F. "The signs and wonders of God are extraordinary, unexplainable, supernatural displays of God's grace witnessed by humanity. Such events are produced by divine _____, for a divine _____, and unmistakably_____ the glory of God" (Dr. Pete Pawelek).

III. While every miracle is a _____ event, not every _____ event is a miracle.

IV. God's signs and wonders are _____.

    A. **Luke 4:40 (CSB)** —⁴⁰ *When the sun was setting, all those who had anyone sick with various diseases brought them to him. As he laid his hands on each one of them, he healed them.*

B. **Acts 8:6–8 (CSB)** — *⁶The crowds were all paying attention to what Philip said, as they listened and saw the signs he was performing. ⁷For unclean spirits, crying out with a loud voice, came out of _____ who were possessed, and _____ who were paralyzed and lame were healed.⁸ So there was great joy in that city.*

C. **John 20:30 (CSB)** — *³⁰Jesus performed _____ other signs in the presence of his disciples that are not written in this book.*

V. **The _____**

    A. They are _____ common than you think.

        1. _____ miracles in the Old Testament.

        2. _____ miracles in the New Testament.

        3. For a total of _____ miracles in the entire Bible.

    B. They are _____ common than we know.

SMALL GROUP QUESTIONS:

1. How did you do with your guess on the number of miracles in the Bible? Did you guess too high or too low? How did you come up with your number?

2. Why do you think many of the signs and wonders of God are *not* recorded in Scripture?

3. If all of God's signs and wonders were recorded in Scripture, do you think anything would be different? If so, how do you think the world would be different if more evidence of the miraculous were revealed in the Bible?

4. Consider the definitions offered in this lesson. As a group, come up with your own definition for the word *miracle*.

5. What bothers you the most about miracles? Before this study, how often did you discuss God's signs and wonders with others? Why?

6. Thinking back on this week's devotional readings, which one surprised you the most? Which one did you find the most interesting? Take some time to discuss your questions or thoughts about the devotional readings with each other as you finish up your group time.

THE IMPULSE OF FAITH

Matthew 14:29 (CSB) — *He said, "Come."*

Read Matthew 14:22–36

The impulse of faith always leads to a true test of reality. That is what we see here in the miracle of Peter walking upon the sea this stormy night. In a perfect reflection of his carnal boldness, Peter's impulse was one of faith: *"Lord, if it's you,"* Peter answered him, *"command me to come to you on the water."*[13] The test of reality, however, was waiting only a few steps away. After seeing the strength of the storm, he started to sink and was forced to cry out, *"Lord, save me!"*

This familiar miracle holds an equally familiar reality for our lives. Like Peter, we have all stepped out amid the great impulse of faith, only to be confronted quickly by the realities of life. Like the disciples, we too understand the fear that comes from a long night at sea. Like these men, we too have thought we were in the place the Lord wanted us to be, and in that very place, we became overwhelmed by the contrary winds of life. It is precisely during these times that we are primed to be pushed out of our comfort zone and into the realm of faith.

Many question the authenticity of this story. Like every miracle in the Bible, it is difficult to wrap your mind around this event. The laws of our universe do not permit humans the ability to walk on water. Yet, here with unlimited ease, Jesus moved effortlessly across the troubled waters of the sea. Some have attempted to explain the miracle by suggesting that the laws of gravity were suspended during this period of time. This comes from our never-ending quest to understand, explain, and rationalize everything. I don't believe the laws of gravity were paused in any way. The truth is simply this: Jesus is stronger and more powerful

---

[13] Matthew 14:28 (CSB)

than any law of the universe. Jesus was the superior force on the sea that night and thus had His way with the storm and the sea.

Consider a strong magnet for a moment. We have all seen, for example, a large magnet attached to a crane pick up and move a vehicle. At that moment, are the laws of gravity suspended? Of course not: the magnet is simply the stronger force and overcomes the laws of gravity. This is the reality that every miracle shows us. God, Jesus, and the Holy Spirit are the superior powers in any and every situation. This is the simplest explanation but remains the answer for every miracle.

Lockyer writes, "when the human mind contemplates the works and ways of God, the question arises, "How can these things be?" Such a query, however, is one of unbelief, not of faith. No wonder should stagger the heart that has learned to trust God and believe in His word. With Him all things are possible."[14] This is what pulled Peter beneath the waves. It was not the power of the storm; instead, it was his doubt, as he wondered, "how can it be that I am walking on the waves?" His great impulse of faith gave way to the reality of the storm. When reality, instead of faith, becomes the superior force in our lives, we are certain to sink beneath the waves of life.

From this miracle, several important lessons emerge. First, even when our faith fails, Jesus remains faithful. Christ didn't abandon Peter in the middle of the storm. He didn't tell him to swim back to the boat on his own. Instead, Jesus lovingly rescued Peter, returned him to the safety of the boat, and then calmed the storm entirely. We may fail but Jesus never will. We must not, however, take this too far and think we can walk on water whenever it pleases us. This miracle doesn't teach us that we should jump up and get out of the boat the instant our impulse to do so arises. Peter had permission to be on the water, and he was clearly called to get out of the boat. Jesus is faithful to rescue us even in

---

[14] Herbert Lockyer, *All The Miracles of the Bible* (Grand Rapids, MI: Zondervan Publishing House, 1961), 202.

our disobedience, but a rebuke is likely to accompany the rescue that finds its foundation in the impulse of disobedience.

It is also comforting to know that even as we struggle against the headwinds of life, and even though we might be tossed and tormented by the waves that pound against us in this troublesome world, Jesus is always there. At times, you may feel forgotten and alone, but you are loved and cherished. Peter sank in familiar waters that he had been given permission to walk upon. You might do this as well, but Jesus will not leave you to fend for yourself or make your own way in life. He is always within arm's reach.

Finally, we are reminded that He is indeed the most overwhelming and superior force. No-one is greater than our Father. Nothing is stronger than our Savior. There is no force in all the universe that can claim dominion over Him. Therefore, we rejoice and walk in great confidence, even into the storms of life. Next time you have the impulse of faith swell up in your spirit, if you hear the voice of God calling you forth, get out of the boat and follow it!

REFLECT—REFOCUS—REPENT—RESPOND

What did you hear God say today?

What will you do with what you learned?

What needs to change?

What questions do you still have?

What will you pray for?

JAWBONE HILL

Judges 15:15 (CSB) — *He found a fresh jawbone of a donkey, reached out his hand, took it, and killed a thousand men with it.*

Read Judges 15:14–20

You have likely heard of the battles of Bunker Hill, Hamburger Hill, San Juan Hill, and Malvern Hill. Or maybe some other lesser-known battles such as the Battle of Crucifix Hill in World War II or the Battle of Halidon Hill, fought in 1333 in the second war for Scottish independence. The Battle for Triangle Hill in the Korean War and the Battle of White Mountain, which took place near the beginning of the Thirty Years' War, may also come to mind. Many of the world's most significant battles have been fought on or over hills, and as a result, they bear these names. But have you ever heard of Jawbone Hill?

Samson's story is one of immense intrigue and misunderstanding. Samson is seen by many as a hero of the faith. There is no doubt that God used him in meaningful and even miraculous ways. However, Samson was full of pride, arrogance, and ego. He is hardly someone to choose as a biblical role model when so many other better options are presented in Scripture. Despite all of his shortcomings, God used this man for His glory. Samson's usefulness is a credit to God, not himself, although Samson might disagree with that statement.

In Judges 15:14, nothing is said about Samson's own strength when his wrists ignited like burned flax and he was miraculously released from his bondage. This was a miracle produced by God, not from the strength or wisdom of Samson. With the Spirit of God upon him, Samson grabbed the fresh jawbone of a donkey and proceeded to kill one thousand men. Being the eldest of four boys, I was in my share of fights as a child. Frequently, I was outnumbered by my younger brothers and cousins in these altercations. Although we never fought to death, I can tell you that getting into a fight with multiple people at the same time can be extremely exhausting, even if you are stronger than your opponents. What God did through Samson this day was nothing short of miraculous.

Following the victory, Samson was thirsty, and he chose to cry out to God. While pleading for water, Samson acknowledged that God had produced this great victory through him but then immediately started to sound like a spoiled child when he said (in verse 18), *"Must I now die of thirst and fall into the hands of the uncircumcised?"* So, the Lord miraculously opened up the ground for Samson to have a drink to quench his thirst.

When I read Samson's story, I'm reminded of how faithful God is and how easy it is for us to become so full of ourselves because of His faithfulness. Samson openly gave God credit for the victory. He knew he couldn't have defeated a thousand men so decisively entirely on his own. He knew that the miraculous work of God was involved in his life. And yet, he almost immediately did two things that are disappointing.

First, like a typical narcissist, he composed a short song to commemorate his victory. He did this in a humorous way that is hard to convey in English translations. In the form of poetic parallelism, he used some word play in the original language. His response "apparently contains a wordplay based on the similar sound of ḥᵃmôr ("donkey") and ḥōmer ("pile" or "heap")."[15] Moore translates this passage like this: "With the bone of an ass, I ass-ailed my ass-ailants."[16] When Deborah won her great battle earlier in Judges 5, her victory was also commemorated in a song. However, she gave all of the credit and glory

---

[15] Herbert Wolf, "Judges," in *The Expositor's Bible Commentary: Deuteronomy, Joshua, Judges, Ruth, 1 & 2 Samuel*, ed. Frank E. Gaebelein, vol. 3 (Grand Rapids, MI: Zondervan Publishing House, 1992), 472.

[16] Herbert Lockyer, *All The Miracles of the Bible* (Grand Rapids, MI: Zondervan Publishing House, 1961), 92.

to God for His miraculous intervention. Samson, instead, chose to retain the glory for himself by recounting what *he* had done to the Philistines.

Next, he decided to rename the place where this miracle had happened. On the surface, the name Jawbone Hill seems appropriate. Military action frequently happens on or around hilltops because of the strategic advantages that topography offers. However, perhaps Daniel Isaac says it best by stating that "the reader might conclude that Samson is hereby naming the geographical site of the victory. That seems *not* to have been the issue here. "Jawbone Hill" apparently refers to the mound he had built with the corpses of the Philistines. Samson does not want to be forgotten!"[17] Samson wanted God's victory through him to be remembered as his own personal victory.

As we consider the supernatural activity of God in our own lives and the victories God has delivered through us, we should be quick to understand our place in the battle. Being an instrument or vessel of the miraculous is far less significant than being the source of the miracle. May we never claim victory, glory, or credit for what God does inside of us, or through us. May our hearts' desire be "Lord, the entire world can forget about me, but may they never forget about you!"

---

[17] Daniel Isaac Block, *Judges, Ruth*, vol. 6, *The New American Commentary* (Nashville: Broadman & Holman Publishers, 1999), 446.

REFLECT—REFOCUS—REPENT—RESPOND

What did you hear God say today?

What will you do with what you learned?

What needs to change?

What questions do you still have?

What will you pray for?

DIVINE TRANSPORTATION

Acts 8:39 (CSB) — *When they came up out of the water, the Spirit of the Lord carried Philip away, and the eunuch did not see him any longer but went on his way rejoicing.*

Read Acts 8

We are first introduced to Phillip in Acts 6:5. He was chosen, along with Stephen, Prochorus, Nicanor, Timon, Parmenas, and Nicolaus, to be a deacon to help the apostles meet the needs of the local church. Little did he know how mightily God would use him for the expansion of the kingdom and what signs and wonders would be delivered through him. Almost immediately, we read, *"Now Stephen, full of grace and power, was performing great wonders and signs among the people."* Phillip and the men confirmed as deacons alongside him might have been chosen to help wait tables, but the Lord anointed them to do far more. While you are likely familiar with the story of Stephen and his martyrdom, most are less familiar with Phillip and his evangelism.

When you think of miracles in the Bible, the name Phillip probably doesn't rise to the top of your list. The eighth chapter of Acts opens with the aftershock of Stephen's death which took place under the leadership of Saul (Paul). The church was under attack, and as a result, it was scattered. Of Stephen, Acts 8:2 recounts, *"Devout men buried Stephen and mourned deeply over him."* It is entirely possible that Phillip was among those devout men who buried Stephen on this day. Following Stephen's murder at Saul's command, the church scattered and Phillip went to Samaria to deliver the good news of the gospel.

During his time there, the Lord produced many miracles through Phillip's ministry. The gospel was clearly the foundation of his message, but the miracles God allowed him to perform were the magnet that got the Samaritans' attention. We are not given many details about the

SIGNS AND WONDERS

miracles he performed. However, Acts 8:6–8 says, *"The crowds were all paying attention to what Philip said, as they listened and saw the signs he was performing.⁷ For unclean spirits, crying out with a loud voice, came out of many who were possessed, and many who were paralyzed and lame were healed.⁸ So there was great joy in that city."*

Here, we see two of the great purposes of many of the miracles we encounter in the Bible. Miracles are hard to miss, and they create a lot of attention. Those who normally would not listen tune in. Not at first because of what they hear but instead because of what they see. This is why the proliferation of miracles is so dense in the life of the early Church.

God's signs and wonders also produce great joy. Even for those who had yet to receive Christ through the message Phillip was preaching, a share of the joy produced by these miracles was available to them. They rejoiced with their friends, family, and neighbors as they were healed and set free from the physical, mental, and emotional limitations they had been slaves to their entire lives.

While these miracles are all of great significance, perhaps the greatest miracle to ever occur in Philip's ministry was that of divine instruction. Although we marvel at the transformation of a sorcerer named Simon and the great works of deliverance done through Phillip's ministry to the Samaritans, perhaps the greatest miracle in his life occurred when the Lord sent an angel to deliver this message, *"Get up and go south to the road that goes down from Jerusalem to Gaza." (This is the desert road.)*[18] How strange the call of God can be. Here, Phillip was commanded to leave behind his fruitful ministry to the Samaritans and walk along the desert road. In full submission and obedience to God, the very next verse says, *"So he got up and went."*

---

[18] Acts 8:26 (CSB)

On that road, he met and eventually led an Ethiopian eunuch who served as the royal treasurer for Queen Candace to the Lord. Following his repentance and transformation by the gospel, this man was baptized by Phillip. Tradition says that this man then took the gospel back to Africa and brought Queen Candace to faith in the Lord. Although this cannot be verified with total certainty, it seems entirely like God to move in this fashion in order to deliver the gospel to a brand-new territory. After all, it was not that long ago that an unknown man named Phillip was selected to be a deacon and then ended up taking the gospel to the Samaritans, accompanied by many signs and wonders.

Following the baptism of the Ethiopian, another miracle happened. The Bible says, *"When they came up out of the water, the Spirit of the Lord carried Philip away, and the eunuch did not see him any longer but went on his way rejoicing. Philip appeared in Azotus, and he was traveling and preaching the gospel in all the towns until he came to Caesarea."*[19] It appears that Phillip was divinely transported to Azotus. This was no trouble at all for the Lord. Indeed, we know that a day is coming when all believers will be miraculously and suddenly transported from Earth to Heaven in the rapture. What a ride this must have been for Phillip. What a ride the rapture is going to be for the Church!

I want to meet this man when I get to glory. We have such a small glimpse into his massive ministry. Eventually, he would settle in Caesarea, and the Lord used him as an evangelist in and around that city for the rest of his life. In fact, approximately twenty years later, Paul, who was formerly known as Saul, would visit. He stayed at Phillip's home while in Caesarea (Acts 21:8). How marvelous and miraculous is the love of God? This is the same man (Saul) who once consented to the killing of Stephen. Stephen was Phillip's friend and a faithful servant of God. The same man who forced the Church to scatter and prompted Philip to

---

[19] Acts 8:39–40 (CSB)

go to Samaria was now greeted as a brother in Philip's home and cherished as a faithful laborer for the Lord. How great is our God?

REFLECT—REFOCUS—REPENT—RESPOND

What did you hear God say today?

What will you do with what you learned?

What needs to change?

What questions do you still have?

What will you pray for?

EARTHQUAKES & ETERNITY

Acts 16:30 (CSB) — *"Sirs, what must I do to be saved?"*

Read Acts 16:25–31

While most believers today are extremely familiar with the exploits of the Apostle Paul, many have only vaguely heard of his companion, Silas. Paul and Peter also refer to Silas as Silvanus (2 Corinthians 1:19, 1 Thessalonians 1:1, 2 Thessalonians 1:1, and 1 Peter 5:12). Silas' name means *"wood"* but more significantly, it was likely chosen to honor the Roman god of *"the countryside"* known by the same name. Paul makes reference to Silas' possible Roman citizenship (Acts 16:37). Like Timothy, it is believed that Silas was a convert to the Christian faith at a young age. We first see him in Scripture (Acts 15:22) at the Council of Jerusalem. According to Acts 15:30–33, Silas was a bold disciple of Christ and a powerful preacher of the gospel. Silas would later be left with Timothy in Berea when Paul departed for Athens. They would rejoin Paul again in Corinth between AD 50–52. Silas would also later accompany the Apostle Peter on his missionary journeys. Much more could be said about this man and his faith, but on this night in Philippi, he found himself suffering in chains for taking part in helping a young slave girl.

Paul and Silas had been forcefully brought into the marketplace and put before the authorities for disturbing the peace. In reality, their only crime was casting a demon out of a slave. The text says in Acts 16:22 that the *"crowd joined in the attack against them and the chief magistrates stripped off their clothes and ordered them to be beaten with rods."* Their beating was not only illegal because they were Romans; the text explicitly says it was severe. They were placed in chains and locked away in the local prison.

Suffering from bleeding backs, extreme bruising, and the dishonor and humiliation brought about by the events of the day, these men could have easily become distraught, worried, or downtrodden in their misery. But instead, as the clock struck midnight, they were found praying and singing songs of praise to God. To my personal shame, I must admit, had I been Paul's companion on this night, he likely would have been singing a solo. What great joy and extraordinary faith we see here from Paul and Silas.

Without warning, a violent miracle took place. Yes, miracles can be violent in nature. On that night, the Lord chose an earthquake as His instrument. This earthquake shook the foundation of the jail. Not only were the doors unlocked; the chains of every prisoner came loose. There is no record of this event causing damage to the jail or to any other surrounding structures, which only enhances how miraculous this event was.

Initially, the jailer believed everyone had escaped, and rather than being held to account for this event, he decided to take his own life. How sad those in his household might have been to find out their father, husband, or son had fallen on his own sword. Yet Paul cried out to the man, *"Don't harm yourself, because we're all here!"*[20] Confirming the truth of Paul's claim, the jailer then asked, *"What must I do to be saved?"*[21]

Jailers in ancient times were not known for their soft, sensitive demeanor. Just the opposite. They were among the toughest, cruelest, and most ruthless men in society. There is little doubt that this jailer was a brute of a man, but on this night, he was transformed into a believer by the greater miracle that is often missed in this account. I'm referring to the miracle of salvation, as he, along with his entire family, were set free from the chains of sin.

On that very night, the jailer and the rest of his household came to believe in the name of Jesus. Indeed, they were baptized, and this former

---

[20] Acts 16:28 (CSB)

[21] Acts 16: 30 (CSB)

brute, who was now a brother, washed the wounds of Paul and Silas. He took the men to his house in the middle of the night, fed them a meal, and rejoiced, because he and everyone in his household received the miracle of salvation. This earthquake had been the catalyst for many to find eternal life in Christ.

One of the most amazing things about God's sovereignty over all creation is His ability to take a terrible situation and use it for His glory. So many times, when we find our backs against the wall of adversity, we pray for God's Holy intervention. We beg for miracles for our own deliverance. Perhaps, instead, we should be singing praises from the deep joy that is within our souls. Fully trusting in the sovereignty of God there, even in the darkness. After all, we serve the King of Kings and Lord of Lords, who can use earthquakes to bring the lost into eternal life.

SIGNS AND WONDERS

REFLECT—REFOCUS—REPENT—RESPOND

What did you hear God say today?

What will you do with what you learned?

What needs to change?

What questions do you still have?

What will you pray for?

THE WALLS CAME DOWN

Joshua 6:17 (CSB) —*Only Rahab the prostitute and everyone with her in the house will live, because she hid the messengers we sent.*

Read Joshua 6:1–27

The miracle that happened at Jericho is not some forgotten miracle. For obvious reasons, it stands alongside other miracles such as the parting of the Red Sea, David's defeat of Goliath, and the resurrection of Lazarus from the dead as being one of the most recognizable miracles in Scripture. Inside this miracle, we find both extreme obedience and transformation.

I have taken excited groups of pilgrims to the site of Jericho on multiple occasions. The portions of the walls that have been excavated and studied are an amazing sight to behold. Jericho is said to be the oldest, most continuously inhabited city in the world. When Joshua and the Israelites approached this city, it was likely the most heavily fortified city in the world. At the heart of the defenses were its walls. If you wish to get a better understanding of what God's people faced and how spectacular this miracle would have been, there are many wonderful artistic renderings of the walls of Jericho online.

In ancient times, Jericho was located in an extremely strategic location. In order for God's people to possess the promised land, this well-fortified city had to fall. The city of Jericho is located in an oasis in the middle of a desert. Even to this day, you will find lush green plants, trees, and other vegetation here, watered by its many natural springs. Jericho was also the gateway to the central highlands of Canaan and, as a result, had to be defeated.

Never before and never since has a fragile, unproven army taken up the strategy employed here. God commanded Joshua and His people to march around the wall for six days in total silence. On the seventh day, they marched around it six times in silence. Then, after marching around one last time, Joshua gave the command to SHOUT. The walls came down, and the city was taken. From this well-known part of the story, we celebrate the value of extreme obedience. That is, no matter how strange God's ways may be, there can only be victory when we obey.

There is, however, a frequently forgotten miracle in this story. Her name is Rahab, and her story is a miracle of transformation. She was a prostitute living within the city walls. She was extremely poor and had been sexually abused and continually taken advantage of, as many women in her day frequently were. She had no material possessions to speak of, and she had absolutely no value to anyone. But she had eyes to see, and she believed in the power of God long before it was put on display. When the two spies Joshua had sent to scout the land and the city were discovered, Rahab put her life on the line to save them. Here is what she said to them: "*I know that the Lord has given you this land and that the terror of you has fallen on us, and everyone who lives in the land is panicking because of you.*"[22] She believed in God's power and the mission His people were on. She helped these two spies escape and safely complete their mission.

When the city's walls fell down and were overrun by the Israelites, Rahab's household was spared, and she was brought out to safety. If her story ended there, that would be enough, but as is often the case, there are multiple aspects of God's miracles. If you look closely at the lineage of Jesus, as reported by Matthew 1, you will find Rahab's name in verse five. She would become the great great-grandmother of King David. Her name is also mentioned in what is commonly known as the "Hall of Faith" in Hebrews 11. Her great faith is also esteemed in James 2:24.

While the miracle of Rahab's transformation is frequently overlooked, it is the greater miracle in this story in my opinion. Through her life, we can see the grace and mercy of God. He took a pagan

---

[22] Joshua 2:9 (CSB)

prostitute and brought her into His family. She was not left outside the camp to follow in the shadows and to exist in the margins. No, God placed her in the middle of Jesus' family tree. From her, we see that God saves and uses people with questionable pasts. While the falling of the stones to the ground that day was extraordinary, it was the transformation of this pagan prostitute's heart of stone into a story of redemption that proves just how miraculous our Father is.

REFLECT—REFOCUS—REPENT—RESPOND

What did you hear God say today?

What will you do with what you learned?

What needs to change?

What questions do you still have?

What will you pray for?

SIGNS AND WONDERS

THE MIRACLES OF GOD

WEEK FOUR

WEEK FOUR: THE SUPERNATURAL

ICE BREAKER

What questions do you ask yourself before you leave the house? Share the list of questions that go through your head when you are getting ready to go someplace.

What is the thing you are most afraid to forget or leave behind when you leave the house? Why?

VIDEO OUTLINE

While every miracle is a _____ event, not every _____ event is a miracle.

I. **Three types of people**

   A. Those who _____ believe in miracles.

   B. Those who _____ know what they believe.

   C. Those who are _____ to believe.

II. _____ **questions to ask**

   A. Is there a _____ or _____ connection to a supernatural agent?

   B. Does the event's overall purpose reveal the person and purpose of _____ _____, or the power, nature, or glory of _____?

SIGNS AND WONDERS

C. Does the event operate _____ of known, proven, and accepted principles of the _____ world?

D. Does the event have a clear and understandable kingdom _____ or _____ at its core?

While every miracle is a _____ event, not every _____ event is a miracle.

SMALL GROUP QUESTIONS:

1. As a group, look over the four questions discussed in this video again. Then take a few minutes to consider a few of the signs and wonders from the Bible and discuss how they line up with each of the four questions.

2. Looking at these four questions, which of the four is the easiest for you to discern or identify when considering if an event is miraculous or not? Which of the four is the hardest to discern or identify?

3. Why do you think it is important to be able to clearly distinguish between events that are supernatural and those that are miraculous?

4. Why do you think our culture so casually uses the word *miracle*? Have you recently called something miraculous as an expression or in some kind of quick reaction? What did you say, and what was the context for this situation? Would you call that event a miracle in light of the four questions in this study? Why or why not?

5. Thinking back on this week's devotional readings, which one surprised you the most? Which did you find the most interesting? Take some time to discuss your questions or thoughts about the devotional readings with each other as you finish up your group time.

THE ROBE

Matthew 14:36 (CSB) —*They begged him that they might only touch the end of his robe, and as many as touched it were healed.*

Read Matthew 14:34–36

Gennesaret is on the western side of the Sea of Galilee. Before the miracles which are the focus of our text today occurred the disciples had been en route to Capernaum before encountering a fierce storm. After being thrown off course, or perhaps after receiving some direction from Jesus that is not mentioned in the text, they came ashore south of Capernaum. Their arrival did not go unnoticed, and before long, a crowd gathered, begging for deliverance. What is unique about this series of miracles during this unexpected visit is the faith displayed.

People in the crowd requested that the sick might touch the end of His robe. That request was granted, and every person who came forth in faith that day was healed. "As a rule, the person with the power to heal would have reached out to touch those who were sick, but these people have such great faith in Jesus that they believe His healing power overflows into the fringe of His garment. There is no hint in the text that Jesus encouraged this belief."[23] There was great faith on display here, and one by one, the sick came to Jesus and were healed.

The healings received were all absolutely life-changing for those who touched His robe. The Greek word used (*diasozo*) is very specific. It carries the weight of complete wholeness. In other words, the text could easily read *"and as many as touched it were made whole."* Or another way to say it would be that the sick were *"completely cured."* Such is the power of Christ. He is not in the business of partial, incomplete, or imperfect

---

[23] Barclay Moon Newman and Philip C. Stine, *A Handbook on the Gospel of Matthew*, UBS Handbook Series (New York: United Bible Societies, 1992), 474–475.

miracles. The work of Christ is always a work of perfection. We can all take great comfort in knowing that whatever work God is attempting to do in your life this very day is a work of absolute perfection.

One of the Bible verses I constantly repeat to myself comes from Paul's encouragement to the Philippians when he declared, *"I am sure of this: that he who started a good work in you will carry it on to completion until the day of Christ Jesus."*[24] Later, he would expand on this idea, proclaiming in Philippians 2:12–13, *"Therefore, my dear friends, just as you have always obeyed, so now, not only in my presence but even more in my absence, work out your own salvation with fear and trembling. For it is God who is working in you both to will and to work according to his good purpose."* How comforting and encouraging it is to know that God is always at work and that His work is always completed with excellence. This is true even outside of God's miraculous works. You do not have to experience a miracle to encounter the power and perfection of His supernatural work.

It is so easy to miss the message when we get wrapped up in the details of the miracle. Matthew does the reader a favor here by not making note of the exact details of the miracles performed on this day. To be certain, they were all life-changing for those who received them. Matthew's message for the reader, however, is about placing our faith, trust, hope, and future in the hands of Christ. It is a message of faith and contentment. Being close to Christ is enough for those who need His touch. To be near the savior in a posture of faith is all that is necessary to receive all that He has to offer.

---

[24] Philippians 1:6 CSB

REFLECT—REFOCUS—REPENT—RESPOND

What did you hear God say today?

What will you do with what you learned?

What needs to change?

What questions do you still have?

What will you pray for?

TREADING ON MERCY

Acts 5:10 (CSB) — *Instantly she dropped dead at his feet.*

Read Acts 5:1–11

Throughout this study, we have primarily highlighted miracles that produced a positive result in the life of groups and individuals. This may lead some to believe that all miracles can be seen in a positive light by everyone. The reality, however, is that many miracles in the Bible resulted in judgment, pain, suffering, and, in some cases, death for the enemies of God. The example in today's reading is one of the most well-known of the so-called negative miracles. However, Ananias and Sapphira hardly stand alone. Herod's death in Acts 12, Elymas the Sorcerer being struck blind in Acts 12, and many of the miracles found in the book of Revelation bring destruction and suffering to the unbelieving world. The miracles that God performed through Moses to force Pharaoh to release His people were utterly disastrous to the land of Egypt. And while we may view miracles such as the walls of Jericho being destroyed and the city being routed as positive, it seems obvious that the inhabitants of Jericho viewed it differently.

All miracles are used by God for the Glory of God, but not all miracles are soft, fluffy, sweet stories. If you don't believe me, consider Ananias and his wife Sapphira. They were, by all accounts in Scripture, saved and committed members of the early Church. This small but rapidly growing community was, according to Acts, of one heart and mind. Some, including Barnabas, had freely chosen to sell their physical possessions and donate the proceeds of the sales to the work that God was doing through the church. It appears Ananias and Sapphira wanted to gain the favor and recognition that those like Barnabas had received, only at a cheaper price. They attempted to fool God, and it cost them their lives. The sudden deaths of these two well-known members of the community brought great fear to everyone else in the church.

Some have attempted to place the blame for their deaths on the Apostle Peter. However, a careful reading of the text reveals that Peter did not actually pronounce any kind of doom or judgment on Ananias. Holding Ananias to account for his sin is far from condemning him to death. No, it was God who called Ananias to answer for His sins with Him face to face that day. Although the text does not say it, it is quite possible that Peter was shocked by the swift action of God, as Ananias lay dead at his feet. Later, Peter said to Sapphira, *"Why did you agree to test the Spirit of the Lord? Look, the feet of those who have buried your husband are at the door, and they will carry you out."*[25] He was again neither casting judgment nor condemning her to death. He did, however, know what God was about to do because of what he saw happen to Ananias some three hours earlier.

This couple was under no obligation to provide all the proceeds from the sale of their land to the church. Their sin was not that they chose to keep some of the money; it was that they chose to do so with the intention of deceit. Why God chose to deal so quickly and severely with these two in this particular situation is not entirely clear. However, like all miracles, it certainly had the effect of getting everyone's attention. The final verse in this passage says, *"Then great fear came on the whole church and on all who heard these things."*

Some may attempt to use this lesson to portray God as an uncaring and evil boogeyman in the sky. That, however, would be wrong because although God dealt with this couple in this way, thankfully, this is not how He regularly deals with liars. If God normally dealt with people this way, I suspect people would be falling over dead in church every weekend. The reality is that God is gracious, patient, and long suffering. His love abounds, and His willingness to forgive is limitless. This, however, gives us no excuse to act like Ananias and Sapphira and trample upon His merciful heart.

---

[25] Acts 5:9 (CSB)

REFLECT—REFOCUS—REPENT—RESPOND

What did you hear God say today?

What will you do with what you learned?

What needs to change?

What questions do you still have?

What will you pray for?

LAUGHING AT THE LORD

Genesis 18:15 (CSB) *But he replied, "No, you did laugh."*

Read Genesis 17:15–22 & Genesis 21:1–6

Laughter is one of the greatest gifts God has implanted into the hearts of humanity. Science has shown that laughter is indeed good medicine. Regular laughter produces positive chemicals for people's physical, emotional, and mental health. Some studies have shown that laughing can actually help you live longer. Proverbs 17:22 says, *"A joyful heart is good medicine, but a broken spirit dries up the bones."* Almost any way you look at it, laughing is a good thing. But have you ever laughed at the wrong time?

I suspect we have all found ourselves in that awkward situation at one time or another. Maybe you laughed too early while a friend was telling a joke. Perhaps it was in a business meeting when you misinterpreted something the boss said as an opportunity for laughter but then discovered you were the only one laughing. We all have a story to tell about a time like this. Now, imagine you laughed at God because you thought something He said was funny. Then God looks at you with a straight face and says, *"What's so funny about that?"* That would be the ultimate awkward moment.

Abraham was one hundred years old and his wife Sarah was ninety when they were told they would have a son. We normally blame Sarah for laughing at God, but in reality, they both chuckled at the thought of this miracle happening in their lives. Genesis 17:17 says, *"Abraham fell facedown. Then he laughed and said to himself, "Can a child be born to a hundred-year-old man? Can Sarah, a ninety-year-old woman, give birth?"* Then later in Genesis 18:12, we find the more famous instance of laughter when the Bible says of Sarah, *"So she laughed to herself: "After I am worn out and my lord is old, will I have delight?"*

Even though people lived much longer in those days, the biblical narrative still declares that Sarah was well past the childbearing age even for women of her generation. The idea of becoming the parents of a new nation is so outrageous that, in and of itself, the promise of God is funny. When you add to it that a miracle of the most extraordinary magnitude would be required for God to pull this off through the womb of a woman who had been barren for almost a century, it's not hard to see why Abraham and Sarah found such humor in God's promise.

The Lord was not done. In fact, like any good comedian, He chose to pile on by instructing the couple to name their son Isaac, which means "*he laughs.*" Each time they mentioned their son's name for the remainder of their lives, they would be reminded of the time they literally laughed at God. It is striking to consider that they found one of the greatest promises of their lives to be so unrealistic that it was funny. The sad thing is, this happens more often than you think.

I can remember being nineteen years old and praying in my dorm room at Texas State University late one Thursday night. I had just finished preaching to a group of about fifty college students at our weekly gathering known as "The Refuge." In a moment of extreme clarity and deep reflection, I felt the Lord whisper into my heart an unbelievable promise. He said, "*One day you will preach to thousands. You will travel the globe telling people about my son. People will read the books I deliver through you. I am just getting started with you.*" I remember chuckling and thinking that this was crazy: I must have had too much Taco Bell for dinner. Like Sarah, I laughed at God. It would, however, be less than five years after that night that I found myself preaching the Gospel in Africa. A short seven years after that evening, I found myself preaching for the first time to over one thousand people who had gathered for a single Sunday service at our church. Eleven years after that night, my first Bible study, "The Absolute Basics of Christianity", was published. Keep in mind that I was a below-average student whose English teacher in high school literally said, "You better join the army because someone as dumb as you are will only be good for catching bullets." Please don't think ill of her; she was frustrated and she has been forgiven. I only share this to express how unbelievable the promises of God can be. We frequently laugh at God, because just like Abraham and Sarah, we forget that nothing is impossible for Him.

Today, I pray that you are reminded of this one truth: if God says it will happen, you can count on it happening. As one commentator noted, "Is a child from a dead womb too marvelous for the One who called all things into existence? It is no laughing matter. He can do it. Nothing is incredible for those in covenant fellowship with the Lord because nothing is too difficult for Him."[26]

---

[26] Allen P. Ross, "Genesis," in *The Bible Knowledge Commentary: An Exposition of the Scriptures*, ed. J. F. Walvoord and R. B. Zuck, vol. 1 (Wheaton, IL: Victor Books, 1985), 59.

REFLECT—REFOCUS—REPENT—RESPOND

What did you hear God say today?

What will you do with what you learned?

What needs to change?

What questions do you still have?

What will you pray for?

TORN

Matthew 27:51 (CSB) —*Suddenly, the curtain of the sanctuary was torn in two from top to bottom...*

Read Matthew 27:45–56

There were two temple curtains, one separating the Jews from the Gentiles—also known as the outer curtain. The other curtain separated the Holy of Holies from the rest of the court. There has been some debate over which curtain of the sanctuary was torn immediately following the death of Jesus. Was it the curtain that separated the Jews from the Gentiles or the curtain that surrounded the inner sanctuary known as the Holy of Holies? Both have major theological implications. Some believe Paul makes a case in Ephesians 2:14 for this event taking place inside the outer curtain: *"For he is our peace, who made both groups one and tore down the dividing wall of hostility. In his flesh,*[15] *he made no effect of the law consisting of commands and expressed in regulations, so that he might create in himself one new man from the two, resulting in peace."* Still others see verses like Hebrews 4:16 as making a case for the torn curtain being the inner dividing wall which represents division between all of humanity and God. While both ultimately lead us to the same conclusion, which is that through the death of Christ, all humanity now has full and free access to God, only one answer can be correct.

The Greek word used here for sanctuary is *naos*. That word settles the issue because it is only used to describe the inner sanctuary of the temple. The veil that was torn was indeed the huge hand-woven curtain that separated everyone from God. Only the high priest was allowed to pass through the veil one time each year to make an atonement for the sins of the people by sprinkling blood on the altar. According to Roman historian Josephus, this massive curtain was predominantly blue and decorated ornately from top to bottom. It was the most recognizable symbol of man's separation from the divine. For thousands of years, it had stood as a symbol of separation. In Exodus 26:31, we read, *"You are to make a curtain of blue, purple, and scarlet yarn, and finely spun linen with a design of cherubim worked into it. Hang it on four gold-plated pillars of acacia wood that have gold hooks and that stand on four silver bases. Hang the curtain under the clasps and bring the ark of the testimony there behind the curtain, so the curtain will make a separation for you between the holy place and the most holy place."*

When Jesus uttered the words *"It is finished"* and took His final breath on the cross, there was no longer any need for this curtain of division. Through the sacrifice of God's own Son, all of humanity now had free and full access to God. No longer would the nation of Israel or anyone else need to depend on a priest for atonement. No longer would the blood of animals be shed in the hope of forgiveness. No longer would a curtain of cloth be used to divide humanity from their loving creator. Indeed, the work was complete. At the very moment Jesus said, *"It is finished,"* God ripped this curtain down in the most miraculous fashion.

Here, in this text, the details are of utmost importance. Matthew is specific in noting that the curtain was torn from top to bottom. This extremely thick hand-woven veil would have been nearly impossible for human hands to tear. So to rip it from top to bottom rather than from bottom to top means the feat could only have been accomplished by God. Some have suggested that this top-to-bottom tearing of the veil shows that God ripped it from Heaven all the way down to Earth, making a way for eternity to become a reality for everyone through Jesus.

How great is our God? Not only did He offer the blood of His own son on the cross for the sins of the world, and not only did He allow the flesh of His son to be torn by the whip, nails, crown of thorns, and spear, but by Himself, He tore down the veil from top to bottom. It was destroyed! Every miracle stands on its own merit as amazing. However, this one that is noted in fourteen short words in Scripture stands out as an extraordinary display of God's grace for you. The writer of Hebrews 4:16 declares, *"Therefore, let us approach the throne of grace with boldness, so that we may receive mercy and find grace to help us in time of need."* This is possible because the veil has been torn.

SIGNS AND WONDERS

REFLECT—REFOCUS—REPENT—RESPOND

What did you hear God say today?

What will you do with what you learned?

What needs to change?

What questions do you still have?

What will you pray for?

SKIN DEEP

2 Kings 5:1 (CSB) —*The man was a valiant warrior, but he had a skin disease.*

2 Kings 5:1–19

The story of Naaman is not the most well known in the Old Testament; however, it carries a great deal of significance and insight into the miraculous nature of God. Naaman was a great man who had proven to be very valuable to the king of Aram. He was respected, powerful, and according to 2 Kings 5:1, used by the Lord to bring victory to Aram. This powerful and popular man, however, had a very big problem: he had leprosy.

Throughout the Bible, leprosy was a common and totally incurable disease. Indeed, some of Jesus' most famous miracles are in His healing of lepers. How or when Naaman contracted the condition is unknown. It appears that his condition had not spread or become extremely advanced because he was still able to carry on his duties as the commander of the king's army. Normally, when we read about someone with this condition, we find them isolated and alone in their suffering. If they were lucky, they might find a group of fellow leapers to live among in their days of pain and suffering. So, how was Naaman able to continue to function? Thomas Constable points out that "In Israel lepers were normally isolated from non-lepers, but this was not always the custom in other nations including Aram. Naaman was able to carry on his duties as long as the disease permitted him to do so."[27] Naaman was not an Israelite, and apparently the custom of Aram allowed Naaman to continue in his service to the king.

---

[27] Thomas L. Constable, "2 Kings," in *The Bible Knowledge Commentary: An Exposition of the Scriptures*, ed. J. F. Walvoord and R. B. Zuck, vol. 1 (Wheaton, IL: Victor Books, 1985), 547.

Aram and the nation of Israel occasionally had military encounters with one another during this period of history. During one of these engagements, it appears that Naaman's army had captured some Israelites, including a young girl who became a slave for Naaman's wife. This young girl then told Naaman about the prophet Elisha in her homeland. It is doubtful that she had ever met Elisha, but she knew of his power. Elisha was known for many things but not for his ability to cure leprosy. In fact, in Luke 4:27, Jesus said, *"And in the prophet Elisha's time, there were many in Israel who had leprosy, and yet not one of them was cleansed except Naaman the Syrian."* This would be a unique miracle if it did occur. The young girl was not certain that healing would be granted, but she was certain that the God of Elisha was able to heal him.

With permission from the king, along with gifts to appease the prophet, Naaman left in hopes of finding a cure for his leprosy. As was the custom of the day, Naaman first approached the king of Israel, who said, "You want me to do what? I can't do that! This is a trick to pick a fight with me!" Elisha heard about this and invited Naaman to seek his healing from God rather than from the king. Wanting the cure, Naaman left at once to find Elisha.

The prophet did not come out to meet with Naaman but instead told him to go to the Jordan River and wash seven times. This infuriated Naaman. The Bible records it this way: *"But Naaman got angry and left, saying, "I was telling myself: He will surely come out, stand and call on the name of the Lord his God, and wave his hand over the place and cure the skin disease. Aren't Abana and Pharpar, the rivers of Damascus, better than all the waters of Israel? Couldn't I wash in them and be clean?" So he turned and left in a rage."*[28] This big man was upset because the prophet would not even come out and meet him. Maybe you have felt this way at some point while seeking help of some kind. The doctor sent the PA in to see you, instead of giving you her own attention. The surgeon had the medical student call you to

---

[28] 2 Kings 5:11–12 (CSB)

report the results of your biopsy. The senior pastor had the associate pastor return your email or phone call. These kinds of things can be frustrating and cause you to become furious like Naaman.

Once again, it was the servants of Naaman who came to his aid. They said to their master, *"You have come all this way, and you were ready to do whatever needed to be done to be healed. If the prophet had asked you to do something hard, you would have done it. But now, because his command is simple, you are upset and refusing?"* Their reasoning was sound, and Naaman did what Elisha had commanded. 2 Kings 5:14 says, *"So Naaman went down and dipped himself in the Jordan seven times, according to the command of the man of God. Then his skin was restored and became like the skin of a small boy, and he was clean."*

The transformation in this text, however, is more than skin deep. After seeing this miracle occur in his life, 2 Kings 5:15 says, *"Then Naaman and his whole company went back to the man of God, stood before him, and declared, "I know there's no God in the whole world except in Israel.""* Paul House argues that "This text contains one of the great Gentile conversion accounts in the Old Testament. Like Rahab (Josh 2:9–13), Ruth (Ruth 1:16–18), and the sailors and Ninevites in Jonah (Jonah 1:16; 3:6–10), Naaman believed in the Lord."[29]

Is your faith only skin deep, or have you turley accepted the reality of God's love and grace in your life?

---

[29] Paul R. House, *1, 2 Kings*, vol. 8, *The New American Commentary* (Nashville: Broadman & Holman Publishers, 1995), 273.

REFLECT—REFOCUS—REPENT—RESPOND

What did you hear God say today?

What will you do with what you learned?

What needs to change?

What questions do you still have?

What will you pray for?

SIGNS AND WONDERS

THE MIRACLES OF GOD

WEEK FIVE

WEEK FIVE: THE PURPOSE

ICE BREAKER

Ask each group member to briefly describe the rarest event they have ever experienced and then answer this question: How did this affect you?

Next, ask each group member to describe the scariest weather event they have ever experienced and then answer the following questions: How did that make you feel? How would you have felt if, in the middle of that weather event, everything was suddenly and miraculously made calm or normal again? How do you think that would affect you?

VIDEO OUTLINE

1) _____ and _____ only to the person receiving the miracle.

2) The effect is _____ lived, and people _____ forget.

   a) **Exodus 14:11–12 (CSB)** —[11] *They said to Moses, "Is it because there are no graves in Egypt that you have taken us away to die in the wilderness? What have you done to us by bringing us out of Egypt?* [12] *Isn't this what we told you in Egypt: Leave us alone so that we may serve the Egyptians? It would have been better for us to serve the Egyptians than to die in the wilderness."*

3) There was _____ or no lasting _____ transformation at all.

SIGNS AND WONDERS

I. They produce _____

II. They produce _____

   A. **Matthew 12:38 (CSB)** —[38] *Then some of the scribes and Pharisees said to him, "Teacher, we want to see a sign from you."*

   B. **Matthew 19:2 (CSB)** —[2] *Large crowds followed him, and he healed them there.*

   C. **Luke 11:16 (CSB)** —[16] *And others, as a test, were demanding of him a sign from Heaven.*

   D. **John 6:26–31 (CSB)** —[26] *Jesus answered, "Truly I tell you, you are looking for me, not because you saw the signs, but because you ate the loaves and were filled.* [27] *Don't work for the food that perishes but for the food that lasts for eternal life, which the Son of Man will give you, because God the Father has set his seal of approval on him."* [28] *"What can we do to perform the works of God?" they asked.* [29] *Jesus replied, "This is the work of God—that you believe in the one he has sent."* [30] *"What sign, then, are you going to do so that we may see and believe you?" they asked. "What are you going to perform?* [31] *Our ancestors ate the manna in the wilderness, just as it is written: He gave them bread from Heaven to eat."*

III. They produce _____

IV. They produce _____

   A. **Matthew 8:27 (CSB)** —[27] *The men were amazed and asked, "What kind of man is this? Even the winds and the sea obey him!"*

   B. **Luke 5:8–9 (CSB)** —[8] *When Simon Peter saw this, he fell at Jesus's knees and said, "Go away from me, because I'm a sinful man, Lord!"* [9] *For he and all those with him were amazed at the catch of fish they had taken.*

SMALL GROUP QUESTIONS:

1. What would you add to this list? Bonus points if your response starts with "A."

2. Why is it so easy for people to dismiss and quickly forget about the miraculous? Why do you think so many people in the Bible remained unconvinced about God, Christ, and later the Church, even though they saw amazing signs and wonders?

3. Consider the text John 6:26–31 again as a group. How do you think Jesus managed this tension throughout His ministry? Do you think there was ever a time when the signs and wonders of God actually became a distraction to the main purpose of His ministry?

4. Why do you think as humans we are so infatuated with and drawn to the miraculous?

5. Thinking back on this week's devotional readings, which one surprised you the most? Which did you find the most interesting? Take some time to discuss your questions or thoughts about the devotional readings with each other as you finish up your group time.

NEVER TOO LATE

Luke 1:13–14 (CSB) —*But the angel said to him, "Do not be afraid, Zechariah, because your prayer has been heard. Your wife Elizabeth will bear you a son, and you will name him John. There will be joy and delight for you, and many will rejoice at his birth."*

Read Luke 1:5–25

The virgin birth of Christ was a miracle. Indeed, it was one of the greatest miracles God ever performed for the sake of humanity. Because of this, the other miracles surrounding the birth of Jesus frequently get forgotten or overlooked. For instance, months before Mary and Joseph were informed of the miracle that would take place in their family, Zechariah and Elizabeth had received the miracle of hope from the depths of their heartache.

Unable to conceive a child early in their marriage, Zechariah and Elizabeth no doubt turned to the Lord in their prayers. They likely sought out the medical advice that could have been offered to them during this period of history. Elizabeth would have almost certainly talked to her mother, aunts, and other women she trusted, seeking counsel and advice over the years. Yet despite everything Zechariah and Elizabeth tried, the days quickly turned to months, the months to years, the years to decades; their youth and any hope of a child of their own faded into the distant past.

But then, Elizabeth conceived. Following the confirmation of her miraculous conception, Elizabeth exclaimed, *"The Lord has done this for me. He has looked with favor in these days to take away my disgrace among the people."* Her barren womb had been a public humiliation that she could never escape from. Their home, void of a child's tears and laughter, had for decades—at least in the minds of Zechariah and Elizabeth—been a source of shame, guilt, and suffering. It was not uncommon at the time for people to associate a person's sins with barrenness. Elizabeth and Zechariah had no doubt felt and experienced the pain of judgment and shame throughout their marriage on account of their inability to have children. This was all over now because their miracle baby would soon arrive, despite the couple being so advanced in years.

When Elizabeth first learned that she was the recipient of this miracle, she automatically believed God had done this great work for her. In her mind, all she could see and understand was that God had finally intervened, and He was removing the disgrace and shame of barrenness that had accompanied her and Zechariah throughout their marriage. However, true miracles are not solely for the benefit of those who receive them. As was the case for Zechariah and Elizabeth and every other recipient of a miracle, God had something much bigger in mind. The miracle, whom they would name John, would be the forerunner for the Messiah. He would pave the way for the ministry of Jesus. He would be the one to baptize Jesus in the Jordan. Later, John would be murdered and become one of the most famous martyrs the world has ever known.

From this miracle, we learn two very important truths. First, miracles are never just for the person who receives them. Miracles are a direct manifestation of the glory of God. Thus, there is always a greater and deeper purpose behind any miracle God chooses to perform. When God intervenes miraculously, it is for His glory and the advancement of His kingdom. We tend to forget this truth because when we read about the miraculous, we automatically place ourselves into the narrative. We think about how we might have felt if we were Zechariah or Elizabeth. We evaluate the miracle based on our own personal experiences that in one way or another parallel the narrative. As a result, we quickly internalize the miracle, and it becomes personal to us. Many times this causes us to expect our own personal miracles, because we become blinded to the eternal purposes of God when we become focused on the personal aspect of the miraculous.

Second, we learn that it is never too late for a miracle. In Luke 1:20, the angel, in speaking to Zechariah, points out that God's timing is always perfect. According to the timeline Zechariah and Elizabeth had for their marriage, the time had long since passed for them to be blessed with a child. However, God waited for the perfect moment to make their dream a reality, not only so John could be a blessing to them but so he could be a blessing to the entire world. While miracles are extremely rare, when they do occur, it's frequently at the last possible moment. The miracles we read about in Scripture are a faithful reminder that when we are at our most helpless or things seem absolutely hopeless, God is still in control and on His throne. It's never too late for a miracle.

SIGNS AND WONDERS

REFLECT—REFOCUS—REPENT—RESPOND

What did you hear God say today?

What will you do with what you learned?

What needs to change?

What questions do you still have?

What will you pray for?

PRESENCE, PROVISION, PROTECTION

Exodus 13:22 (CSB) —*The pillar of cloud by day and the pillar of fire by night never left its place in front of the people.*

Read Exodus 40:34–38

At the end of their first day's march out of Egypt, God appeared with a great source of protection and provision for his liberated people. For 430 years, the people of God had been held captive in Egypt. During this time, the Lord had not spoken to His people. It was a period of deep divine silence. How refreshing it must have been for them to feel the presence of God literally leading them out of their bondage. Yet due to their years of captivity, they were absolutely unprepared for the journey ahead. It is not an overstatement to note that their journey would have been impossible without God's provision and protection. For the next forty years, they would witness a miracle all day every day and all night every night: a pillar of fire by night and a pillar of cloud by day.

While Moses is widely considered to be the leader that took God's people through the wilderness, God actually did most of the leading. The Lord went ahead of His people in the cloud by day and in the pillar of fire by night. When the Lord stopped, His people stopped. When the Lord moved, they moved. There was no-one in the camp who at any time could not look up and see the presence of God in their midst. It is hard to imagine how incredible this would be: to wake up and go to sleep each day and be able to see the symbol of God's presence watching over you.

There was undoubtedly a practical side to God's provision as well. His guidance would ensure that His people never lost their way. He could guide them through the terrain and on their journey far from hardened enemies such as the Philistines. This miracle also made it possible for

SIGNS AND WONDERS

God's people to travel at night if need be. In the glow of God's grace, they could walk around the camp long after the sun was gone from the horizon. On the coldest nights, this pillar of fire may have provided warmth for God's people. By day, they could find shelter from the immense desert heat in the shadow of the cloud. Imagine what others must have thought. There is little doubt that many would-be attackers likely changed their minds after considering what power these wandering nomads possessed, since this cloud and pillar of fire were always with them wherever they went.

While the cloud by day and pillar of fire by night have long disappeared, the presence, provision, and protection of God for His people have not. Today, we have the Holy Spirit to guide us on our journey in life. Time and time again in Scripture, we are assured that we need not worry, because our father in heaven cares about us. We are promised that He will never leave, forsake, or abandon us. Although much has changed in the years between the Israelites' departure from Egypt and today, the Lord has not! He is as faithful to us today as he was to those walking with Moses out of slavery toward the promised land. Let us rejoice in the presence, provision, and protection that God brings to our lives each and every day.

REFLECT—REFOCUS—REPENT—RESPOND

What did you hear God say today?

What will you do with what you learned?

What needs to change?

What questions do you still have?

What will you pray for?

THE FIRST

John 2:11 (CSB) —*Jesus did this, the first of his signs, in Cana of Galilee. He revealed his glory, and his disciples believed in him.*

Read John 2:1–11

Due to the silence of Scripture concerning the first three decades of Jesus' life, many scholars, theologians, priests, preachers, and lay people have attempted to fill in these years with what have become nothing more than myths and legends. One of these is that Jesus was a miracle worker throughout His youth. There are many who believe that as a young boy, Jesus did miracles and performed wonders for all those in His community to see.

Some use today's Scripture passage as the basis for their belief. The prompting of His mother in the text leads them to presume that she was aware of His power. Some say that this is why she asked Jesus to use His power for the benefit of those attending the wedding. However, John 2:11 settles the matter, pointing out that this was actually the first of the miracles that Jesus performed. It is not that the power to do such things had not lived inside Him throughout His life. Rather, the divine discipline of Christ allowed Him to contain it until His Father in Heaven called for it to be unleashed. If one can accept that Jesus never once sinned, even in His youth, then it is not hard at all to believe that He was disciplined with His miracle-working power as well.

As MacArthur points out: "The miracles Jesus performed constitute one of the most powerful and convincing proofs of His deity."[30] So it comes as no surprise that here, after His testing in the wilderness, and the calling of His first disciples, that the time has come for the world to

---

[30] John F. MacArthur Jr., *John 1–11*, MacArthur New Testament Commentary (Chicago: Moody Press, 2006), 76.

see the power of God through His one and only son. Why at a wedding feast? This question is one we may never know the answer to. Initially, Jesus refused His mother's request for intervention in the situation. However, somehow and in some way that we are not privileged to know, God revealed that the time had come for the miraculous works of Christ to begin.

The miracle had the desired effect. The text says that following the miracle *"his disciples believed in him."* Some level of belief already existed in their hearts for them to accept the call of discipleship. This miracle, however, put them on notice that Christ was indeed who he said he was. The manifestation of God's glory in front of their eyes and eventually on their lips removed whatever doubt they may have had when they arrived at the wedding celebration concerning Jesus.

I don't think it's by accident that this first miracle of Christ is one of great transformation. The time required to make a fine wine is measured in years, not minutes. Yet here Jesus took ordinary water and turned it into extraordinary wine through the force of His divine will alone. He did not wave a hand, touch the jars, or stir the water with His holy finger. He simply instructed the servants to fill the jar to the brim with water, then draw it, and as a result everyone could taste and see that the Lord is good.

This first miracle of Christ is a reminder for all believers in the spiritual discipline of submission. Mary submitted when Jesus first refused to help. Those who gathered the water fully submitted to this strange request to fill the jars to the brim with water. Each of the six jars would have held twenty to thirty gallons of water. Filling the jars was no small task, and at the onset, it likely seemed like an exercise in futility. However, they obeyed fully and did what they were asked by Jesus. Once the miracle occurred, I am quite certain they were glad they had filled those jars to the top. The submissive hearts of these and others who witnessed or received miracles through the ministry of Jesus can't be overstated. May our hearts be filled to the brim with obedience as we follow Jesus ourselves.

REFLECT—REFOCUS—REPENT—RESPOND

What did you hear God say today?

What will you do with what you learned?

What needs to change?

What questions do you still have?

What will you pray for?

CONVINCINGLY UNCONVINCED

Exodus 4:13 (CSB) —*Moses said, "Please, Lord, send someone else."*

Read Exodus 4:1–16

If you have ever been reluctant to step out and fulfill the mission God has placed on your heart, then you're in good company. The pages of Scripture are full of men and women who displayed a great deal of hesitation, resistance, and outright defiance when faced with the call of God. Even one of the greatest leaders in the Old Testament was initially extremely reluctant to submit his life to God's calling.

Moses lived one hundred and twenty years. As a baby, his life was spared by providence—in part thanks to his mother's and sisters' efforts to save him from the extermination edict of Pharaoh. Namely, Pharaoh had commanded the midwives to kill any male Hebrew child who was born. Moses' mother hid him for several months before placing him in a basket and floating him down the Nile, where he was found by one of Pharaoh's daughters. For the next forty years he lived in Egypt. He then fled to Midian after he murdered an Egyptian after observing him beating another Hebrew. Moses would remain in a self-imposed exile in Midian for the next forty years. The final forty years of his life are what we generally celebrate Moses for today. It was during these years that he was used as God's instrument to lead the Hebrews from Egypt to the banks of the promised land. During this Exodus, God would manifest His miraculous power over forty times through Moses' life. There are an additional sixteen miracles that happened in the presence of Moses during these years. There is no other human agent of the miraculous who can match both the quantity and awesomeness of the miracles performed during Moses' lifetime.

Moses is described as God's servant in places such as Numbers 12:7 and Joshua 8:31. In Psalms 106:23, Moses is described as God's chosen one, and in 1 Chronicles 23:14, Moses is called "the man of God." In the Christian Standard Bible (CSB), the name of Moses appears 820 times in 775 verses. In comparison, the name of Jesus appears 948 times in 911 verses. H.H. Halley calculated that the story of Moses accounts for approximately one seventh of the entire Bible.[31] Anyway you look at it, the life of Moses played a crucial role in God's story. However, he almost refused the call of God altogether.

While tending his flock in Midian, Moses came upon a bush that was burning but would not burn up. After hearing God's voice, experiencing a burning bush that did not burn, witnessing two miracles, and being promised a third miracle, Moses said, "*Please, Lord, send someone else.*"[32] There was absolutely no doubt in Moses' mind that he was the wrong man for the job. He was convincingly unconvinced that he was capable of fulfilling his assigned mission, even with the promise of divine help from the Lord.

From this text, we learn something important about miracles. Many times, we ask for signs and wonders to confirm what God's direction is. We pray that God will intervene and deliver a miracle, and then we will certainly be ready to fulfill our mission. However, the Bible reveals that this rarely happens. Most people are just like Moses. Even when confronted with the miraculous, they remain unconvinced. After Moses finally accepted his calling and returned to Egypt, Pharaoh remained convincingly unconvinced that God's people should be set free, even though he witnessed miracle after miracle. After witnessing the parting of the Red Sea, eating manna from heaven, and seeing numerous other miracles, the nation of Israel wanted to kill Moses, the very man through

---

[31] Herbert Lockyer, *All the Miracles of the Bible* (Grand Rapids, MI: Zondervan Publishing House, 1961), 43.

[32] See Exodus 4:13 (CSB)

whom God had performed these miracles. Their deepest desire as a group was to return to Egypt so they could be slaves, rather than face the wilderness and march into the Promised Land. As another example, Esther was an orphan in a foreign land. Her miracle came when, by the power and sovereignty of God's grace, she became queen. Still, she struggled to step up to her calling. Until the very last minute, Esther remained unconvinced that she could make a difference. In the same way, consider all of the people, including the Pharisees, who witnessed miracle after miracle during the ministry of Jesus. Those who shouted, *"Crucify Him. Crucify Him. Crucify Him"* had all seen or at the very least heard about the miracles of the Messiah, but they, too, remained convincingly unconvinced.

Are we any different today? Are you any different? Many people want to experience the miraculous because they feel that the manifestation of a sign or wonder of God in their life will confirm what they are seeking. However, time and time again, the biblical narrative contradicts this assumption.

Chances are, there is something in your life that you are convincingly unconvinced about right now. Even after you have experienced the greatest miracle of all—the forgiveness of your sins and the power of the resurrection and of the Holy Spirit living inside of you. However, you still won't go, you still won't lead, you still won't give, you still won't speak, you still won't share the gospel. The reality is that you still won't do whatever it is you know God wants you to do because you are convincingly unconvinced. Perhaps today is the day you need to fully embrace the activity of God in your life and step up or step into His calling and purpose in faith. Stop waiting for a sign and start obeying God's commands.

God patiently and gently dealt with Moses' anxiety and apprehension. While Moses' journey toward his purpose and calling started with him being a doubtful deliverer, eventually he accepted his calling and pressed into the will of God wholeheartedly. May we not remain unconvinced that God can do something amazing through our lives. Instead, let us embrace the call of God and walk into the future with great faith.

REFLECT—REFOCUS—REPENT—RESPOND

What did you hear God say today?

What will you do with what you learned?

What needs to change?

What questions do you still have?

What will you pray for?

GET UP AND GO

Luke 17:19 (CSB) —*And he told him, "Get up and go on your way. Your faith has saved you."*

Read Luke 17:11–19

During what would be His last pilgrimage to Jerusalem, Jesus and His disciples passed through Samaria and encountered a band of ten lepers, who were bound by nothing more than their common misery. This dreaded disease had put all ten of these men on a level playing field. In the past, they may have had vastly different social statuses. Some may have been rich and others poor. Some may have been blessed with families and others single. On this day, though, they found themselves at the mercy of Jesus, as they suffered alone in the company of each other.

While the main symptoms of leprosy are well known, its effect on the voice is not so well known. Those suffering from this disease develop a persistent cough and extreme hoarseness, making it difficult to talk. Luke was a physician by profession, and, as such, he noted something most readers miss in this miracle, an important detail that signifies a total healing: *"But one of them, seeing that he was healed, returned and, with a **loud voice**, gave glory to God."*[33] This is in contrast to the first encounter, when all ten of the leapers raised their fragile hoarse voices together and said, *"Master have mercy on us!"*

The lepers initially did not approach Jesus to make their request to be healed. Rather, they stood at the prescribed distance of one hundred feet to ensure they could not infect others. Interestingly, Jesus never touched them, nor did he offer any blessing or word of healing. Indeed, Christ offered no assurance of healing at all. Instead, he issued a simple instruction for all ten men to depart and show themselves to the priest.

---

[33] Luke 17:15 (CSB)

This priest possessed no power to heal the men, but by their law, had the power to pronounce them clean. Only once they were pronounced clean could they return to their families and return to a normal way of life.

As the lepers left to do what Christ commanded, gradually the physical distance between them and Jesus increased. However, God's mercy and goodness followed them, for while they were on their way, the miraculous happened. They were healed. This is a powerful reminder for all believers that our Father is not limited by distance. We are never far away from a miracle, because the Master of all miracles is always with us.

While nine of those in this group continued on their way upon discovering they were healed, one turned around and came running back to Jesus. We are told he was a Samaritan. Although he had initially wandered away from Christ when consumed by this wretched disease, he now ran in his clothing of rags as fast as possible to give thanks. Overcome with gratitude, this Samaritan cast himself at the feet of Christ to give glory to God.

While the other nine lepers had the faith to be healed, it seems that only this one had the faith required for salvation. After having his physical healing confirmed, Jesus bestowed another great gift of mercy on the Samaritan. This man had come to realize who Jesus really was, and as a result Jesus said, *"Get up and go on your way. Your faith has **saved** you."*[34] This man not only received the miracle of the restoration of his physical health; he also became the recipient of a new life free from sin when the sun set on this day. This was not a result of the leper's gratitude but of the Lord's grace. This man was not just cleansed of leprosy; he was cleansed of all his sin and unrighteousness by placing his faith and trust in Jesus.

---

[34] Luke 17:19 (CSB)

This unknown, unnamed man had his name written in the Lamb's book of life that day. He serves as a good example for each of us. Whether or not we receive our physical, financial, medical, or other earthly miracles, Jesus is the greatest Miracle of all. We should put our hope and trust in Him alone.

SIGNS AND WONDERS

THE MIRACLES OF GOD

WEEK SIX

WEEK SIX: WHO PERFORMS MIRACLES?

ICE BREAKER:

Let each group member share their thoughts about the following questions before getting started with today's lesson: First, as a child, how did you view God? What were the major characteristics of God that you focused on in your youth or early years as a believer? How has your understanding of God changed over time? How do you view Him now?

VIDEO OUTLINE

I. _____

    A. Is there a _____ or _____ connection to a supernatural agent?

        1. Supernatural _____

        2. Supernatural _____

    B. **Matthew 13:57–58 (CSB)** — *⁵⁷And they were offended by him. Jesus said to them, "A prophet is not without honor except in his hometown and in his household."⁵⁸And he did not do many miracles there because of their unbelief.*

    C. **Exodus 8:19 (CSB)** — *¹⁹"This is the finger of God..."*

    D. **Matthew 14:32–33 (CSB)** — *"Truly you are the Son of God."*

SIGNS AND WONDERS

II. _____ _____

    A. **John 20:30 (CSB)** —³⁰ *Jesus performed many other signs in the presence of his disciples that are not written in this book.*

III. The _____ _____

    A. **Acts 2:4–8 (CSB)** —⁴ *Then they were all filled with the Holy Spirit and began to speak in different tongues, as the Spirit enabled them.⁵ Now there were Jews staying in Jerusalem, devout people from every nation under heaven.⁶ When this sound occurred, a crowd came together and was confused because each one heard them speaking in his own language.⁷ They were astounded and amazed, saying, "Look, aren't all these who are speaking Galileans?⁸ How is it that each of us can hear them in our own native language?"*

    B. **Romans 15:18–19 (ESV)** —¹⁸ *For I will not venture to speak of anything except what Christ has accomplished through me to bring the Gentiles to obedience—by word and deed,¹⁹ by the power of signs and wonders, by the power of the Spirit of God—so that from Jerusalem and all the way around to Illyricum I have fulfilled the ministry of the gospel of Christ.*

IV. _____

V. _____ of_____

    A. **Acts 19:11 (CSB)** —¹¹ *God was performing extraordinary miracles by Paul's hands.*

VI. The _____ and _____ **Spirits**

    A. It's _____

    B. It's _____

    C. It's _____

i. **2 Thessalonians 2:9 (CSB)** —⁹ *The coming of the lawless one is based on Satan's working, with every kind of miracle, both signs and wonders serving the lie.*

ii. **Revelation 13:11–14 (CSB)** —¹¹ *Then I saw another beast coming up out of the earth; it had two horns like a lamb, but it spoke like a dragon.*¹² *It exercises all the authority of the first beast on its behalf and compels the earth and those who live on it to worship the first beast, whose fatal wound was healed.*¹³ *It also performs great signs, even causing fire to come down from heaven to earth in front of people.*¹⁴ *It deceives those who live on the earth because of the signs that it is permitted to perform in the presence of the beast, telling those who live on the earth to make an image of the beast who was wounded by the sword and yet lived.*

iii. **Revelation 16:13–14 (CSB)** —¹³ *Then I saw three unclean spirits like frogs coming from the dragon's mouth, from the beast's mouth, and from the mouth of the false prophet.*¹⁴ *For they are demonic spirits performing signs, who travel to the kings of the whole world to assemble them for the battle on the great day of God, the Almighty.*

iv. **Matthew 24:24–25 (CSB)** —²⁴ *For false messiahs and false prophets will arise and perform great signs and wonders to lead astray, if possible, even the elect.* ²⁵ *Take note: I have told you in advance.*

SMALL GROUP QUESTIONS:

1. Do you think it's possible for a miracle to happen without supernatural authority and supernatural power? Explain your position.

2. Do you think it's possible for God to perform a miracle in the absence of faith? Why or why not?

3. As a group, spend some time talking about the theological implications of the Devil having the authority and power to perform signs and wonders. How does this make you feel?

4. Have you ever considered that Jesus never used His authority or power for Himself? What does that say about Jesus? Why do you think He never once used His authority or power to perform a miracle for His own benefit? How does this make you feel?

5. Have you ever felt or seen the supernatural power or supernatural authority of God at work in or through your life? Share some examples with your fellow group members and rejoice in the ways God has allowed each of you to be used for His glory.

6. Thinking back on this week's devotional readings, which one surprised you the most? Which did you find the most interesting? Take some time to discuss your questions or thoughts about the devotional readings with each other as you finish up your group time.

BURIED BY GOD

Deuteronomy 34:6 (CSB) — *He buried him in the valley in the land of Moab facing Beth-peor, and no-one to this day knows where his grave is.*

Read Deuteronomy 34:1–8

Lockyer writes of the miracles of Moses, "To no other mortal has there been granted the high privilege of being the agent of so many and such stupendous displays of supernatural power. Moses lived in the atmosphere of the miraculous and his end accorded with his life." Moses' final moments in life were accompanied by a miracle, and even in his death, we find the Miracle Maker Himself at work.

Before he drew his final breath, God convened with Moses one last time. On this occasion, God granted him the miracle of supernatural vision. The Bible says he went up from the plains of Moab to Mount Nebo, and *"the Lord showed him all the land."* Mount Nebo is located about twenty-five miles southwest of present-day Amman Jordan. Although I've never been to its peak, I have seen it many times on our trips to the Holy Land from the shores of the Dead Sea. At almost 12,000 feet high, if you know where to look, it is not hard to spot. It's from this peak that God allowed Moses to see what he would never touch or taste himself. The Promised Land.

Miraculously, God allowed Moses to look to the north some one hundred and fifty miles. He then looked elsewhere and was allowed to see the beautiful Mediterranean Sea, the Negev, Manasseh, and much more. We don't know how long this took or exactly how it happened. As with many of the miracles we encounter in Scripture, we are left to ultimately trust God in the details. However, we do know that Moses was able to view these places with *"his own eyes."* Even from the vast height of Mount Nebo and with perfect vision, it's impossible to see this far without supernatural vision. As the leader of God's people, Moses had endured much. He had been faithful, and now, on his last day as a mortal man, God was faithful to show Moses the fruits of his labor, although Moses would never taste them himself.

The English version of the Bible we read then says, *"So Moses the servant of the Lord died there in the land of Moab, according to the Lord's word."*[35] More literally, the Hebrew says it the way the Rabbis like to express it: Moses died with "the kiss of the Lord." At the age of one hundred and twenty years, this great man of God departed Earth for eternity. But then something totally unexpected and unique happened. The Lord Himself, we are told, buried Moses.

Of everyone we see pass away in Scripture, only Moses was buried by God. The Lord lovingly takes his servant and lays him to rest in a secret place known only to Himself. It is a tender and touching gesture performed by a present and loving Father. In Jude 9, we are told that God's archangel Michael fought the Devil himself over the body of Moses. We know that Moses' body was transfigured in the presence of Jesus and three of his disciples, so it is easy to conclude who won that fight.

For most of his life, Moses was the agent of God's miraculous work. Here, on the final day of his life, he became the lone recipient of these two miracles. From this text in Deuteronomy, we take comfort knowing that God cares for His servants from the very beginning to the very end. He is sovereignly and equally faithful while knitting us together by Himself in our mother's wombs and as we draw our final breath and transition into eternity.

---

[35] Deuteronomy 34:5 (CSB)

REFLECT—REFOCUS—REPENT—RESPOND

What did you hear God say today?

What will you do with what you learned?

What needs to change?

What questions do you still have?

What will you pray for?

INFINITE REACH

Luke 7:9 (CSB) — *"I tell you; I have not found so great a faith even in Israel."*

Read Luke 7:1–10

Normally, when a miracle occurs in Scripture, the medium by which the miracle is initiated or achieved is some kind of physical interaction. It might be a touch, saliva used to make mud (which is then rubbed into the eyes of the blind), or a voice command. In this passage however, something very special happened. Jesus did not touch, see, or physically encounter the one being healed at all. This particular miracle is a sign and symbol of the infinite reach of Christ.

Only Matthew and Luke record this miracle in their gospel accounts. Each of them offer their own perspective on the events. Matthew, who writes to a primarily Jewish audience, highlights different things compared to Luke, who writes primarily to a Gentile audience. Luke offers more details regarding the miracle in this passage and the events leading up to it as well. These details point to some extraordinary layers of this miraculous work.

For example, in Luke 7:3, we learn that initially the centurion sent some of the Jewish elders to find Jesus and request His help. It is a well known fact that Jews did not respect the Romans. The relationships between the Jews and Roman officers like this centurion were hostile and filled with bitterness. For too long, the Jews had lived under the yoke of Rome. Mistreatment and abuse were common, and it was the officers who directed their soldiers to inflict pain and abuse on the Jews and many others under Roman rule. For these reasons and many more the Romans were despised by the Jews.

Knowing this, one might think the Jewish elders were dispatched by force. Perhaps this Roman officer sent them to find Jesus under compulsion or threat. However, Luke 7:4 provides us with the details to

SIGNS AND WONDERS

show that it was out of love and respect for this man that these elders went to solicit Christ's help. The Bible tells us this centurion had built a synagogue for the Jews. While centurions were paid modestly well, they were not known for spending their wealth on Jews. It is extraordinary to find this kind of respect and admiration during this period of history between these foes.

This Roman officer also seems to have genuine respect not only for the Jewish people but for Jesus as well. He humbly later told Jesus not to come to his house because he was unworthy to have someone such as Christ under his roof. He admitted that he had sent the elders because he felt unworthy to approach Jesus himself and ask for the miracle that was needed to save his servant. Then the centurion sent word and said, *"Lord, don't trouble yourself, since I am not worthy to have you come under my roof. That is why I didn't even consider myself worthy to come to you. But say the word, and my servant will be healed."*[36] Recognizing Christ as the authority of all things, he believed this miracle was possible without the presence, touch, or even vocal affirmation of Jesus.

Many people were amazed by Jesus. His parents were amazed (Luke 2:33), His disciples were amazed(Matthew 8:27), the crowds were amazed (Matthew 9:33, Mark 9:15), Pilate was amazed (Mark 15:5), and even the Pharisees were amazed at times(Matthew 22:15-22). However, here we are told that Jesus was amazed by this man's understanding of His authority and by the faith that was on display in his request. It is no small thing to amaze the Son of God. Jesus praised this Gentile's faith and said, *"I tell you, I have not found so great a faith even in Israel."*[37]

No promise of healing is recorded; the touch of Christ was never felt upon the servant's flesh, but in Luke 7:10, we learn that the servant was fully healed. Here, we see that the reach of Christ is infinite. No distance

---

[36] Luke 7:6-7 CSB

[37] Luke 7:9 CSB

could stop the healing power of Jesus. But the infinite reach of Christ is displayed even more powerfully, in that this Gentile Roman centurion was not out of reach of the gospel. On this day, those present witnessed pride, prejudice, and hundreds of years of polluted relationships disappear, as the despised Jewish Rabbi named Jesus was amazed by the faith of a Roman centurion.

REFLECT—REFOCUS—REPENT—RESPOND

What did you hear God say today?

What will you do with what you learned?

What needs to change?

What questions do you still have?

What will you pray for?

THE SUN STOOD STILL

Joshua 10:13 (CSB) —*And the sun stood still and the moon stopped until the nation took vengeance on its enemies.*

Read Joshua 10:1–27

Unlike his predecessor, Joshua was not a leader through whom the Lord performed many miracles. In the book of Exodus, for example, we find no fewer than twenty-two miracles performed under Moses' leadership. In the entire book of Joshua, we find only three. These are the parting of the waters of the Jordan; Jericho's walls falling down; and the sun standing still in its place for an entire day.

One of the things about this miracle that most people forget is that the sun and moon were both principal deities for the Canaanites. How terrifying it must have been for the enemies of Israel to see the sun and moon stand still in the sky above them as *"the Lord fought for Israel."* This event was also recorded in other places outside of the Bible. The biblical text itself makes reference to *"The Book of Jashar,"* which is mostly a collection of songs that honor the great accomplishments of Israel's leaders. Additionally, "the apocryphal book called *The Wisdom of Sirach* (Ecclesiasticus) states, "Was it not through [Joshua] that the sun stood still and one day became as long as two?" (*Sir* 46:4, NRSV), and Josephus likewise claimed that this day was longer than the ordinary day (*Ant.* 5.1.17).[38] There are many different theories about what happened on this day. As with most miraculous events, many have expended great effort to explain these events away.

It is easy to see why so many can't believe in a God who performs miracles like these. Most people can't even cause the faucet to stop

---

[38] David M. Howard Jr., *Joshua*, vol. 5, *The New American Commentary* (Nashville: Broadman & Holman Publishers, 1998), 241.

dripping, so trying to comprehend the suspension of the universe is simply unimaginable. However, we are reminded that just because we can't do something doesn't mean that God is limited as well. It would not be any harder for God to stop the sun and moon than it is for a conductor to stop a train or for a pilot to stop a plane. It would be no harder for God to stop the day than it is for you to stop your vehicle or turn your computer off. He is the Creator, and He is in total control of all creation.

However, many disagree, saying that if God had indeed stopped the sun and moon, the entire world would have fallen apart. For example, opponents of the miraculous say that tidal waves and other cosmic events would have occurred all over the world if God had stopped or slowed down the rotation of the earth. Of course, in our limited understanding of how the universe works, these thoughts are justified. However, as the supreme Creator, God would have had no problem prohibiting the sea or any other part of creation from destroying His creation.

While many proposals have been made regarding this miraculous manifestation of God's power and love, I find the simplest explanation to be the most likely. That is, Joshua asked God to do something, and God did it. God, in some miraculous way, stopped the Earth from rotating or slowed its rotation significantly on this day. This is the view of Augustine, Jerome, Luther, Calvin, and many other theologians. The sun and moon stood in obedience to their Creator as God fought for Israel on this day.

Whether it can be proven or not is not of utmost importance for those who walk in faith. All that matters is that we understand that we serve a mighty and miraculous Master. The lesson here is simple as well. If the sun and moon stand still in obedience to God, so should we.

REFLECT—REFOCUS—REPENT—RESPOND

What did you hear God say today?

What will you do with what you learned?

What needs to change?

What questions do you still have?

What will you pray for?

AN UNWELCOME MIRACLE

2 Chronicles 26:16 (CSB) —*¹⁶ But when he became strong, he grew arrogant, and it led to his own destruction.*

Read 2 Chronicles 26:15–21 & 2 Kings 15:1–7

When most people think of miracles, they automatically think of good things happening. They think of someone's cancer being healed. Perhaps they think of a friend who received a miraculous pay rise or promotion. Maybe they think of someone who walked away from a terrible automobile accident without a scratch. These and many other positive events form the foundation for what most people consider miraculous. These kinds of events would not be definable as signs and wonders biblically, but they remind us of the positive impression we have of the miraculous. The Bible, however, shows us time and time again that God can use miracles in ways that negatively impact people as well.

Uzziah assumed the throne at the tender age of sixteen, and his reign spanned fifty-two years. He is considered one of the few good kings that Judah had. As the leader of God's people, he was successful in battle against their enemies. He strengthened the defenses around the cities and was responsible for the works to create large cisterns to collect rainwater for his people. He rebuilt ports and established trade routes across the known world. 2 Chronicles 26:8 says, *"His fame spread as far as the entrance of Egypt, for God made him very powerful."* Under his leadership, the towers and walls of Jerusalem were restored. He is described as a *"lover of the soil"* and was a king who helped the farmers and vinedressers by digging wells and making other provisions so that they could be more productive.

Then we read these tragic words, *"But when he became strong, he grew arrogant, and it led to his own destruction."* In the early years of Uzziah's life and reign as king, he had been fully dependent on God. The Lord had provided for him and made him prosperous, popular, and powerful. But

SIGNS AND WONDERS

Uzziah, like many both before and after him, allowed this all to go to his head. In his mind, he was invincible, and the attitude of invincibility inevitably led to his destruction.

Puffed up with pride and overflowing with arrogance, Uzziah made his way to the Lord's sanctuary and attempted to offer incense on the altar. The priest Azariah and no fewer than eighty other priests stood against Uzziah and told him what he was doing was wrong. Uzziah knew that only the descendants of Aaron had the right to bring incense before God. Even as a king who had been appointed and blessed by God, he did not have the right to approach the altar or offer a sacrifice to God.

Uzziah did not listen and pressed ahead with his plan. Then, a most unwelcome miracle occurred. As he approached the altar, leprosy broke out on his forehead. The Bible tells us that he never was healed. He carried this disease for the rest of his life and was forced to live in seclusion until the time of his death. His son Jotham took over the day-to-day duties of governing the people.

King Uzziah's unwelcomed miracle is similar to that of Moses' older sister Miriam, who was struck with leprosy due to her own pride (Numbers 12:10–15). She, however, was healed seven days later and was not forced to suffer her entire life like Uzziah did. These are only two examples of many miracles that were surely unwelcome events for people in Scripture. From these two examples, we learn several valuable lessons.

First, we are reminded that God is both sovereign and just. He is a God of accountability, and a Father who will not spare the rod, especially in the life of spoiled children such as Uzziah and Miriam. From an earthly perspective, some of the miraculous things that happen are not always positive for those that experience them. However, from a spiritual perspective, they can facilitate our return to faithful service and renewed passion and focus for the kingdom of God.

It should also be obvious that both spiritual pride and presumption should be avoided in the life of a Christ follower. Both Uzziah and Miriam expressed signs of extreme pride before they were overcome with leprosy. They both presumed they could do or say anything they wanted and get away with it. This, however, is never the case with God. There is nothing He does not see, and there is no-one who is beyond His reach.

Finally, Uzziah's tragic story should remind us of the seriousness of sin. He never recovered, nor did he ever regain his ability to act in full capacity as king. All this was due to the pride and arrogance that swelled up inside of him and overtook him on the day he entered the sanctuary, only to leave him with the mark of this most unwelcomed miracle. May we all heed the advice offered in Proverbs 16:18: *"Pride comes before destruction, and an arrogant spirit before a fall."*

REFLECT—REFOCUS—REPENT—RESPOND

What did you hear God say today?

What will you do with what you learned?

What needs to change?

What questions do you still have?

What will you pray for?

A UNIQUE MIRACLE

Luke 22:51 (CSB) *And touching his ear, he healed him.*

Read Luke 22:47–53

Every miracle in the Bible brings its own level of uniqueness. The miracle performed by Jesus in restoring a man's ear, however, stands out to me. This miracle is nothing more than a passing detail for many, mostly due to the extreme nature of the situation in which it occurs. The magnitude of what is happening and what is about to happen to Jesus takes center stage, and this healing of a man's ear is almost forgettable compared to the other events that are unfolding around it.

Judas had betrayed Jesus, and an armed cohort of guards had come to arrest Him. The intense time of prayer in the garden was interrupted by the sound of armor and weapons clanging through the still night air as the guards approached the garden. Peter reacted with his normal impulsive nature by drawing his sword and cutting off part of the ear of the chief priest's servant. Had his aim not been so poor, we might have seen Jesus bringing another person back from death rather than only restoring his ear.

The event is recorded in all four of the gospels; however, only John gives us the name of the servant who was struck. His name was Malchus. Interestingly, John is also the only one to tell us explicitly that Peter dealt the blow. Certainly, the other gospel writers knew who did it, but they don't provide that detail. Luke was a doctor and, as a man interested in medical details, he is the only gospel writer to tell us that Jesus healed the man's ear. The account is short and contains little detail in all four of the gospel accounts but by combining them, the reader can gain a better understanding of what happened that night.

In Luke 22:38, we learn that there were only two swords in possession of the disciples that evening. When Jesus was threatened,

Peter put his to use, and its intended effect was death. However, Jesus used the opportunity to perform his last healing miracle. What makes this miracle of healing unique is not that it was the final one. Rather, it is filled with unique details that set it apart from all the other miracles of Christ.

For example, unlike many of the other healings Christ had performed, this miracle apparently required no faith or even desire on the part of the recipient. In the other accounts of Christ's healings, the recipient, a parent, or friend possessed both desire and faith and as a result were granted their healing. Here, Jesus did not wait for either desire or faith on the part of Malchus or anyone else to offer the restoration of this man's flesh.

Furthermore, this miracle was granted to an enemy of Christ who had not expressed any kind of repentance for his actions. Malchus was there as a part of the group that would arrest Jesus. While Christ had a window into the heart of Malchus that we do not, there's no indication that the miracle was offered as a result of Malchus' change of heart in regard to Jesus. Indeed, this man was an enemy of Christ when he arrived and appeared to remain so at the time of his healing.

It seems almost fitting that the last miracle Jesus would perform before dying on the cross would be for a man with no faith or desire to be healed and who was labeled an enemy of Jesus. On the cross, Jesus would heal the wound of sin on behalf of the entire world. Here in the garden, he touched and healed the physical wound of an enemy. One commentator wrote so wonderfully about this event. "His (Jesus') method of conquering force was by submission; violence, by meekness; sin, by the cross. He wins His victories, not by a sword but by His scars."[39]

---

[39] Herbert Lockyer, *All The Miracles of the Bible* (Grand Rapids, MI: Zondervan Publishing House, 1961), 240.

Although it is tempting to believe that the only miracle here is the restoration of a man's ear, the true miracle is the willingness of Christ to help Malchus at all. He had not earned, nor did he deserve, the Lord's help. Furthermore, he never requested Jesus' help, and still Christ reached out in love and made this sinner's flesh whole again. In the same way, Jesus still reaches out in love and makes the souls of sinners whole again in love to this very day. Not because we have earned it, deserve it, or even because we ask for it. Rather, it is only the supremacy of His love and grace that provides the miracle of transformation and eternal restoration to each of us.

SIGNS AND WONDERS

REFLECT—REFOCUS—REPENT—RESPOND

What did you hear God say today?

What will you do with what you learned?

What needs to change?

What questions do you still have?

What will you pray for?

SIGNS AND WONDERS

THE MIRACLES OF GOD

WEEK SEVEN

WEEK SEVEN: MODERN MIRACLES

ICEBREAKER

Have each group member answer the following question. If time and money were not a factor, which of the following would be your preferred transportation method for a long journey? Explain your answer.

a. Personal vehicle

b. Train

c. Bus

d. Airplane

e. Cruise ship

f. Walking

g. Horseback

VIDEO OUTLINE

They Produce_____

They Produce_____

They Provide _____

They Produce_____

SIGNS AND WONDERS

I. **This is** _____

   A. God uses signs and wonders primarily for His_____ not our individual _____.

II. **Miracles from _____ Feet**

   A. Miracles in the Old Testament establish the _____ of God.

   B. Miracles of Christ establish His claims to _____ and _____.

   > i. **Luke 5:20–26 (CSB)** —²⁰ *Seeing their faith he said, "Friend, your sins are forgiven." ²¹ Then the scribes and the Pharisees began to think to themselves, "Who is this man who speaks blasphemies? Who can forgive sins but God alone?" ²² But perceiving their thoughts, Jesus replied to them, "Why are you thinking this in your hearts? ²³ Which is easier: to say, 'Your sins are forgiven,' or to say, 'Get up and walk'? ²⁴ But so that you may know that the Son of Man has authority on earth to forgive sins"—he told the paralyzed man, "I tell you: Get up, take your stretcher, and go home." ²⁵ Immediately he got up before them, picked up what he had been lying on, and went home glorifying God. ²⁶ Then everyone was astounded, and they were giving glory to God. And they were filled with awe and said, "We have seen incredible things today."*

   > ii. **Matthew 14:32–33 (CSB)** —³² *When they got into the boat, the wind ceased. ³³ Then those in the boat worshiped him and said, "Truly you are the Son of God."*

   > iii. **John 20:30–31 (CSB)** —³⁰ *Jesus performed many other signs in the presence of his disciples that are not written in this book. ³¹ But these are written so that you may believe that Jesus is the Messiah, the Son of God, and that by believing you may have life in his name.*

C. Miracles of the Apostles establish the _____ as a divine institution.

III. What about _____?

SMALL GROUP QUESTIONS:

1. Before this study, did you think miracles were more common or less common than you do now? What has changed?

2. Do you think it helps to look at the miracles of the Bible from a 30,000 foot perspective? Why or why not? How does this change the way we view the signs and wonders of God?

3. What are some of the similarities and differences you see in God's signs and wonders through the progression of Scripture? What stands out to you from Old Testament miracles, the miracles of Christ, and the miracles of the Apostles? What do they have in common and what changes?

4. If you could pick one miracle in the Bible to witness yourself, which one would it be and why?

5. As a group, take some time to share any modern-day miracles you may have heard about, read about, or even seen with your own eyes. How can you be certain they are indeed miracles?

6. Thinking back on this week's devotional readings, which one surprised you the most? Which one did you find the most interesting? Take some time to discuss your questions or thoughts about the devotional readings with each other as you finish up your group time.

A LINE IN THE SAND

Daniel 3:18 (CSB) — *"But even if he does not rescue us, we want you as king to know that we will not serve your gods or worship the gold statue you set up."*

Read Daniel 3:8–30

On March 6, 1836, the defenders of the Alamo in San Antonio, Texas, were massacred by Santa Anna and his army. Sometime before this final battle, Colonel William Travis, the commander of the defenders of the Alamo, is believed to have drawn a line in the sand. Santa Anna had sent word that they would take no prisoners and that the fate of anyone inside of the walls was sealed. Santa Anna gave all of the defenders one last opportunity to lay down their weapons and save their lives. Travis drawing a line in the sand gave everyone a choice: "If you cross this line, you will stay and defend these walls with your life." Tradition says that all but one stepped across that line in the sand.

In the book of Daniel, we discover three young men who themselves faced a similar moment. Hananiah, Mishael, and Azariah were friends of Daniel and faithful followers of God. They are better known today as Shadrach, Meshach, and Abednego. King Nebuchadnezzar was not a soft or sensible man. He ruled his kingdom with an iron fist, like most of the kings of the world do. He had previously issued a decree declaring that *"everyone who hears the sound of the horn, flute, zither, lyre, harp, drum, and every kind of music must fall down and worship the gold statue."*[40] Hananiah, Mishael, and Azariah were followers of God and had no intention of worshiping any king or idol he had set up.

It is important to note that Hananiah, Mishael, and Azariah had a lot to lose. They had been given positions of authority by King Nebuchadnezzar. After Daniel interpreted Nebuchadnezzar's dream in

---

[40] Daniel 3:10 (CSB)

Daniel 2, he got a promotion. Daniel then requested that the king appoint Hananiah, Mishael, and Azariah to help him manage the province of Babylon, and that request was granted. These four boys were likely in their late teens or early twenties when all of this occurred. They had lots of life in front of them, and they were in positions of influence and power. All they had to do to hold onto all of this was cross this line in the sand and bow down and worship this statue.

This, however, was a line they could not cross. So, some Chaldeans brought malicious accusations against Hananiah, Mishael, and Azariah, likely out of jealousy. The king gave them one final chance to bow down and worship, and they refused. Their punishment would be death by burning, and their fate was sealed.

One of the greatest lessons we learn from this miracle comes from the response Hananiah, Mishael, and Azariah give to Nebuchadnezzar. Like many people, King Nebuchadnezzar chose to believe in God when it was convenient for him. Daniel 2:46–47 says, *"Then King Nebuchadnezzar fell facedown, worshiped Daniel, and gave orders to present an offering and incense to him. The king said to Daniel, "Your God is indeed God of gods, Lord of kings, and a revealer of mysteries, since you were able to reveal this mystery."* He was convinced of God's supremacy and ultimate power, yet here in Daniel 3, the king was puffed up with pride and asked, *"And who is the god who can rescue you from my power?"*

Hananiah, Mishael, and Azariah did not even answer the question. They simply gave this reply, "If the God we serve exists, then he can rescue us from the furnace of blazing fire, and he can rescue us from the power of you, the king. But even if he does not rescue us, we want you as king to know that we will not serve your gods or worship the gold statue you set up."[41] Although no doubt existed in the minds of Hananiah, Mishael, and Azariah about the ability of their God to deliver them, they humbly accepted the fact that God does not always choose

---

[41] Daniel 3:17–18 (CSB)

to intervene miraculously in human circumstances, even on behalf of His most faithful servants.⁴² Sometimes, the miracle does not come, as the defenders of the Alamo each found out as they drew their final breath upon those fateful walls.

The same is true for us. While we can be certain that we serve a God of miracles, we are not guaranteed that miraculous intervention will happen in our lives. There is a line in the sand, and I pray you find the courage to step across it. Not because you believe you will receive a miracle, but because you understand that the Master of miracles loves you deeply and is worthy of your faithful submission to His will.

---

⁴² Stephen R. Miller, *Daniel*, vol. 18, *The New American Commentary* (Nashville: Broadman & Holman Publishers, 1994), 119.

REFLECT—REFOCUS—REPENT—RESPOND

What did you hear God say today?

What will you do with what you learned?

What needs to change?

What questions do you still have?

What will you pray for?

GOD'S SOVEREIGNTY

Acts 12:2 (CSB) —*and he executed James, John's brother, with the sword.*

Read Acts 12:1–19

As believers, the goal is not so much to understand the miracle or even the Miracle Maker Himself. Rather, our goal is to realize that our Father in heaven is sovereign over everything, including our lives. A deeper and more disturbing reality for many is that His sovereignty does not always produce the results we desire, as we see here in Acts 12.

In this chapter, we are confronted with the mystery of God's selective purpose. In back-to-back reports, we learn of James' martyrdom and Peter's miraculous rescue and release. James walked into prison and was then killed by the sword. Peter, on the other hand, walked in just like James, but God sent an angel from Heaven to rescue him and lead him out. In our minds, one was abandoned, and one was rescued; however, a more mature view of the situation is that both were rescued. Indeed, one can argue that James got the better end of the deal.

Campbell Morgans says, "It may remain to us a perplexing question why James was slain and Peter delivered. There is no explanation. Nevertheless, the revelation of the facts is assuring. That God delivered Peter proves His power to have delivered James. That He did not deliver James proves that the death of James was within the compass of His will, and we know that in the great unveiling all will be seen to have been right."[43] We will never know the mind or heart of God fully enough to understand why His servant, James, died in his chains while Peter was

---

[43] Herbert Lockyer, *All The Miracles of the Bible* (Grand Rapids, MI: Zondervan Publishing House, 1961), 278.

released from his. We do, however, know that we can trust the sovereignty of God.

Peter's situation seemed hopeless from the perspective of man. While knowing of James' fate, Peter is bound in chains and flanked by multiple guards to ensure he can't escape. There are guards at the door, guards inside his cell, and guards literally chained to the Apostle. Even here, against these most impossible odds, we find the Church at work. While Peter was sleeping, the faithful were praying. Herbert Lockyer says that "constant contact with the miraculous had taught them (the church) to believe that what was impossible with man is possible with God. So, the church gave themselves to continued, intense, and earnest prayer."[44]

Peter's ultimate trust in the sovereignty of God is on display here as well. The Bible records that he was sound asleep when his miracle was initiated. While lesser men would have been filled with anxiety, despair, and fear, Peter was sound asleep, knowing that God was in total control. The miracle of his rescue and release from prison is nothing less than spectacular. It shows just how easy it is for God to exercise His power over humanity and inanimate things, such as prison doors. With great ease and no resistance at all, the angel of God ushered Peter to his freedom.

It is with this same ease that God ushered James to his eternal freedom as well. There is no way to understand why the sovereignty of God called James home and Peter to more service. The reality, however, is that the same God was in control of both of their lives. The same God, this very day, is in control of yours. This is why, as followers of Christ, we do not place our hope in miracles but rather in the God who initiates and performs them.

---

[44] Ibid. 278

REFLECT—REFOCUS—REPENT—RESPOND

What did you hear God say today?

What will you do with what you learned?

What needs to change?

What questions do you still have?

What will you pray for?

INFINITE PROVISION

1 Kings 17:14 (CSB) —*The flour jar will not become empty and the oil jug will not run dry…*

Read 1 Kings 17:8–16

It can be easy to forget that our God is infinite in every way. The miracle of infinite provision found in chapter seventeen of 1 Kings is a prime example of how our Father sustains us. In this great illustration of faith, we find much to celebrate and pursue as believers.

It should be clear to you by now that God's source of provision is rarely found in the place you would most expect it. In this miracle, the Lord says to Elijah, *"Get up, go to Zarephath that belongs to Sidon and stay there. Look, I have commanded a woman who is a widow to provide for you there."*[45] Geographically, this was not the most convenient or safest option for the prophet. Zarephath was a village located about a mile off the Mediterranean coast between Tyre and Sidon. It was approximately eighty to ninety miles north of the wadi, where the Lord had been sustaining Elijah. However, the wadi had dried up due to the drought and famine, so it was time to move. On his journey north, Elijah must have wondered, "Why is the Lord sending me to Zarephath?" Zarephath was the homeland of Jezebel and the heartland of Baal worship. This seems like the most unlikely place for the prophet to find the provision needed to sustain his life and ministry.

The Lord was also specific about directing Elijah to be on the lookout for a local widow who would provide for him upon his arrival. During times of drought, famine, and hardship in Elijah's day, widows were normally the first to run out of food, as they were, almost without exception, among the poorest in ancient society. They rarely had enough

---

[45] 1 Kings 17:9 (CSB)

SIGNS AND WONDERS

food and supplies to care for their own needs, much less the needs of strangers. However, walking in faith, Elijah pressed on toward his destination.

Many attribute Elijah's faith to the miracle in this passage. However, the heart of this lonely widow was known by the Lord, too. We are not told her entire story. She was absolutely alone, raising her son all by herself. Then, she encountered this stranger asking for food and water. Initially, at Elijah's request, she offered him some water from the little she had. Then, the prophet asked for food, and she exclaimed, *"I don't have anything baked: only a handful of flour in the jar and a bit of oil in the jug."*[46] Elijah then learned that she had been gathering firewood to make the last meal for herself and her child. This widow carried the weight and expectation of death by starvation following this final meal. Elijah then told her to make him some bread first, and she would be able to tap into the infinite provision of God. In faith, she did what was asked, and indeed day after day, her flour jar did not become empty, nor did her oil jug run dry.

Perhaps you can relate to this widow's plight. It seems we have all gone through seasons of life at one point or another where it took everything we had to just hang on to the knot at the end of the rope. Maybe you are a widow, widower, or single parent. Is your bank account dry or quickly evaporating? Are the circumstances of life overwhelming? If you are in this kind of desperate situation, put your faith in the hands of God. He loves and cares for you more than you can possibly imagine. You are not alone, and the creator of the universe will never abandon you!

As modern-day disciples, we should both celebrate and pursue the kind of faith we see here in this widow's life. We should always remember that our Father in Heaven is a God of infinite provision. This doesn't mean we will never face hard times, or that we will always live a life of

---

[46] 1 Kings 17:12 (CSB)

physical abundance. It does, however, mean that there's nothing we need that He is not able to provide. While neither her jar nor jug ever ran *over*, the real point was that they never ran *out*. So many times, we seek the miracle of abundance rather than accepting what the God of infinite provision lovingly provides. When we cease looking for abundance and humbly open our eyes to God's provision, we are certain to be pleased with what we find.

REFLECT—REFOCUS—REPENT—RESPOND

What did you hear God say today?

What will you do with what you learned?

What needs to change?

What questions do you still have?

What will you pray for?

THE CONFUSED WIDOW

1 Kings 17:23 (CSB) — *Elijah said, "Look, your son is alive."*

Read 1 Kings 17:17–24

Yesterday, we looked at the miraculous provision the Lord provided for Elijah and this poor widow. Through the Lord's infinite power and grace, her jar and jug never ran dry. Yet we later find this same widow's life left totally empty, as she suffers unimaginable pain at the loss of her only son. Her plight can only be fully known by those who have experienced such tragedy themselves.

This is the first recorded instance of a physical restoration of life in the Bible. Upon hearing her son take his last breath, this widow likely could not even entertain the possibility of ever seeing her son alive again. She had likely never heard of anyone coming back to life, and since our expectations are so strongly shaped by our experiences, from her perspective, this was hopeless. Elijah had never raised anyone from the dead before, and, like the widow, he probably did not even consider the possibility initially.

Despite the miracle that had taken place previously with the jar and jug, both the widow and Elijah expressed their doubt and disappointment in God. The widow cried out in her pain, *"Man of God, what do you have against me?"* She was convinced that God was punishing her for past sins. Sometime later, Elijah would also cry out to the Lord. He said in his own anguish over the situation, *"Lord my God, have you also brought tragedy on the widow I am staying with by killing her son?"*[47] They were both confused by this tragedy that took place in the middle of their miracle.

---

[47] 1 Kings 17:20 (CSB)

As far as we know, Elijah had never attempted to bring anyone back to life before. Rather than just placing his hand on the boy, he stretched himself out over the child. It did not work the first time. Or the second. However, he was persistent in his faith and in his prayer, crying out, *"Lord my God, please let this boy's life come into him again!"*[48] And from this state of panic, pain, and confusion, the Lord miraculously restored this child's life.

Something that is easy to miss when you're reading about miracles in the Bible or from other accounts is that they don't always solve every problem in someone's life. It is easy to read about Jesus healing the blind, lame, or leprous and get the impression that the miracle made everything in their lives better. Without a doubt, in that moment, the biggest problem of their lives was solved. However, we can be assured that life presented more problems to each of them in the days that followed their miracle moment. Even after the Red Sea was parted and the Israelites ate manna from Heaven, the issues of life in the wilderness were still there. Miracles don't always make everything better, but they do always point us to the One who holds everything in His hands.

Another obvious reality is that miracles don't always arrive. Indeed, in the entire Bible, there are only ten accounts of resurrection miracles. We are never promised or guaranteed that the miraculous intervention of God will save the day in our situation. This reality, however, should enhance our faith, not cause it to evaporate. There's no denying that it's far easier to trust God for a miraculous healing than to trust Him in the brokenness that accompanies bereavement. It's more desirable to trust God for the miraculous restoration of our marriage, rather than in our singleness. Most would find it far more desirable to experience miraculous success or victory—even over His spiritual grace that supernaturally sustains us in our suffering. The point here is that God is

---

[48] 1 Kings 17:21 (CSB)

no less faithful in the absence of the miraculous. You can trust God with or without receiving His miraculous intervention.

We tend to evaluate events like this one with the widow's son from the perspective of what actually occurred. Perhaps a better way to view this is to consider what would have been different if the miracle never happened at all. Certainly it's easy to imagine how tragic and terrible this would have been for the boy's mother. Her life would have never been the same. However, if this miracle never took place, would it have changed the nature, character, or compassion of God even a little bit? Of course not!

My point is this: even in the absence of a miracle from God, we still serve a marvelous Master. He is able to sustain us even when no miracle is offered. This is why our hope should always be firmly placed in the Lord Himself, not miracles. Our hearts should echo that of the Psalmist in saying, *"Now, Lord, what do I wait for? My hope is in you."*[49]

---

[49] Psalm 39:7 (CSB)

SIGNS AND WONDERS

REFLECT—REFOCUS—REPENT—RESPOND

What did you hear God say today?

What will you do with what you learned?

What needs to change?

What questions do you still have?

What will you pray for?

MIRACLE MACHINE

Mark 8:23 (CSB) — *"Do you see anything?"*

Read Mark 8:22–26

In my mid-thirties, while on the first deer hunt of the season, I noticed that I couldn't see clearly through my rifle scope. Initially, I thought the scope had accumulated dust during the months of inactivity since the previous season. But after cleaning the scope, I looked through it again, only to discover that it was still very blurry. In fact, I couldn't make anything out. Frustrated, I concluded that something had happened to my scope and that it would need to be replaced. When the hunt was over that evening, I had someone else take a look through the scope. They reported that it was normal, and everything looked perfectly fine. It was at this point that I closed one eye and discovered that I couldn't see anything clearly out of my left eye.

I didn't know it at the time, but the human eye is an amazing work of God's grace. One of our eyes will actually compensate for the other in the event that something happens. In my case, even though both eyes were open, my mind had started to use only my right eye for all of its vision needs. I would soon learn that I was legally blind in my left eye and didn't even know it. After a series of tests, the optometrist determined that I'd developed a cataract in my left eye. This was brought on as a side effect of a medication I'd taken in the previous year to help battle a series of sinus infections. After my cataract surgery, I reported to the optometrist's office the following morning for my follow-up appointment. The optometrist removed the patch that had been placed over my eye the day before, following the surgery. As I opened my eyes, I couldn't believe how bright and clear everything was. After a quick eye test, it was confirmed that literally overnight, I'd regained perfect 20/20 vision in my left eye again.

While my situation and that of the blind man here in Mark 8 have very little in common, I can, on some level, understand what he might have felt after being healed by Jesus. The ability to see clearly is one of the many things we frequently take for granted, but it is vital in so many ways. Mark's gospel is the only one that records this specific miracle of Christ. There are three items of particular interest in this miracle.

First, notice that some friends or family members took this blind man to Jesus. It was not uncommon for others to take people to Jesus for healing. We aren't told the names of those who took time out of their day and made an effort to get their friend into the presence of Christ. But the reality is that they cared about this man, and they knew the miracle he needed could only be found in the presence of Jesus. How much more should we long to ensure that everyone we care about and love is brought to Christ to receive the miracle of salvation? As friends and family of those who remain spiritually blinded by Satan, we should do everything we can to bring our friends into the presence of Jesus so that they can be set free from their spiritual blindness and walk in the light of Christ.

Jesus did two very interesting things in this miracle. First, He took the man by the hand and led him outside of the village away from the crowds. In general, Jesus' miracles were performed in public for everyone to witness. However, three times (Mk. 5:35–43; 7:31–37; 8:22–26) in the gospel of Mark, it is noted that Jesus took those who were to receive the miracle away from the crowds. It seemed that people had come to think of Jesus as something of a miracle machine. Here, Jesus reminded the crowds and this man that this was not the case. By taking the man out of the crowd, Christ revealed how deeply relational His miracles are.

The final and perhaps most interesting thing about this miracle is that the man was not instantaneously healed. After spitting in his eyes, Jesus asked the man, *"Do you see anything?"* The man responded and essentially said, "I can see something. I see people: they look like trees."

He could see them moving, but his vision was not clear enough to really see. Then Jesus placed His divine hands of healing upon the man's eyes again, and the text says his sight was restored. Why did Christ do this? Obviously, this man could have been fully healed on the first attempt but wasn't. We may never know the full intent behind the two-stage process in this miracle. Perhaps part of the lesson is that it is very possible to see but not see clearly. There are many today who have blurry, cloudy, spiritual eyes. They can vaguely see the ways of Jesus but still largely remain blind. Like me with my cataract, they don't even know how poor their vision is because they have had blurry or blinded spiritual vision for so long.

Does that describe you? Have things become cloudy or blurry? Is there a time in your past when you recall being able to hear and see the things of God much more clearly? If so, take some time today and ask Jesus to restore your spiritual vision.

REFLECT—REFOCUS—REPENT—RESPOND

What did you hear God say today?

What will you do with what you learned?

What needs to change?

What questions do you still have?

What will you pray for?

SIGNS AND WONDERS

THE MIRACLES OF GOD

WEEK EIGHT

WEEK EIGHT: COMMON QUESTIONS

ICE BREAKER

Discuss the following question as a group: If you could ask God to change one problem in the world today, what would you ask for and why?

VIDEO OUTLINE

Let's Connect:

1. Website: www.pastorpete.org.

2. Facebook: @cfpastorpete

3. Twitter: @cfpastorpete

4. Instagram: pastorpetepawelek

5. Youtube: Pete Pawelek

I. Is it ok for me to ask God to _____ a miracle?

   A. **Matthew 12:38–39 (CSB)** —[38] *Then some of the scribes and Pharisees said to him, "Teacher, we want to see a sign from you."*[39] *He answered them, "An evil and adulterous generation demands a sign, but no sign will be given to it except the sign of the prophet Jonah."*

SIGNS AND WONDERS

    B. **Luke 23:8–9 (CSB)** —*⁸ Herod was very glad to see Jesus; for a long time he had wanted to see him because he had heard about him and was hoping to see some miracle performed by him.⁹ So he kept asking him questions, but Jesus did not answer him.*

    C. **1 Corinthians 1:22–23 (CSB)** —²² *For the Jews ask for signs and the Greeks seek wisdom,²³ but we preach Christ crucified, a stumbling block to the Jews and foolishness to the Gentiles.*

    D. **Matthew 24:23–25 (CSB)** —²³ *"If anyone tells you then, 'See, here is the Messiah!' or, 'Over here!' do not believe it.²⁴ For false messiahs and false prophets will arise and perform great signs and wonders to lead astray, if possible, even the elect.²⁵ Take note: I have told you in advance."*

II. If God can heal _____, why doesn't He heal _____?

    A. **John 5:3–6 (CSB)** —³ *Within these lay a large number of the disabled—blind, lame, and paralyzed.⁵ One man was there who had been disabled for thirty-eight years.⁶ When Jesus saw him lying there and realized he had already been there a long time, he said to him, "Do you want to get well?"*

1. God has the _____ choice to deal with one, _____ , or _____.

    A. **Romans 8:31–32 (CSB)** —³¹ *What, then, are we to say about these things? If God is for us, who is against us?³² He did not even spare his own Son but gave him up for us all. How will he not also with him grant us everything?*

2. A person's eternal _____ is more important than their temporary _____.

III. Is God's miraculous activity a _____ of increased _____ or_____ ?

A. **Ephesians 2:1–5 (CSB)** —*[1]And you were dead in your trespasses and sins[2] in which you previously walked according to the ways of this world, according to the ruler of the power of the air, the spirit now working in the disobedient.[3] We too all previously lived among them in our fleshly desires, carrying out the inclinations of our flesh and thoughts, and we were by nature children under wrath as the others were also.[4] But God, who is rich in mercy, because of his great love that he had for us,[5] made us alive with Christ even though we were dead in trespasses. You are saved by grace!*

B. **John 3:16–18 (CSB)** —*[16] For God loved the world in this way: He gave his one and only Son, so that everyone who believes in him will not perish but have eternal life.[17] For God did not send his Son into the world to condemn the world, but to save the world through him.[18] Anyone who believes in him is not condemned, but anyone who does not believe is already condemned, because he has not believed in the name of the one and only Son of God.*

SMALL GROUP QUESTIONS:

1. What are the dangers of seeking signs and wonders as proof of our faith or God's favor on our lives?

2. Do you think it is ok to ask God to perform a miracle? Why or why not?

3. Why don't you think God grants all of our prayer requests, especially those that are critical and require His miraculous intervention? What if He did miraculously intervene and grant every request we made? What would that actually look like?

4. Have you ever thought God had placed more favor on someone else? What are the dangers of thinking like that? Do you think it is possible for God to love someone else more than He loves you?

5. What is the most important thing you learned during this study? How has this study impacted your life?

6. Thinking back on this week's devotional readings, which one surprised you the most? Which did you find the most interesting? Take some time to discuss your questions or thoughts about the devotional readings with each other as you finish up your group time.

7. Are you willing to take one to two minutes of your time and complete this short survey? Scan the QR code below or use the link to be directed to the online survey.

SHORT ONLINE SURVEY

www.pastorpete.org/signs-wonders

GRUESOME & GLADSOME

Exodus 7:23 (CSB) — *Pharaoh turned around, went into his palace, and didn't take even this to heart.*

Read Exodus 7:14–25

The great Nile River was the center of Egyptian civilization. This river was the source of both its economic and religious life. In the days of Moses, Egyptians believed that the Nile was the gateway to the afterlife. In the ancient Egyptian religion, Osiris was the god of fertility, agriculture, the afterlife, the dead, resurrection, life, and vegetation. The Egyptians believed that the Nile was directly connected to Osiris' bloodstream. Making this miracle performed by God was even more symbolic and meaningful.

The Egyptians had several other gods that were tied to the waters of the Nile. Hapi, also known as Apis, was the bull god of the Nile. Isis was one of the Egyptian goddesses of the Nile, and Khnum was the god whom Egyptians believed was the guardian of the Nile. Other Egyptian gods were tied to fish, floods, and other aspects of the Nile. The Nile River was a big deal to the Egyptians, and it would be the canvas upon which God would reveal some of His most memorable miracles. Each of the ten plagues performed by God through Moses and Aaron was a direct attack on the worthless gods of the Egyptians. While we can read through all ten miracles in a few minutes in our Bibles, these events most likely took place over about nine months.

God first turned the water of the Nile into blood. Fish are not created to live in blood, and as a result of this miracle, they all died. This was a major food source for the Egyptians. Thus, in one miracle, God brought about both thirst and hunger for the people of Egypt. The sight and smell produced by this horrific event are hard to imagine. It was so bad that the Egyptians could not drink from the river. Some have suggested that the Hebrews had stopped drinking from the Nile long before this, since its waters were used to kill their children by the order of Pharaoh. As a result of God turning the water in the river to blood, the Egyptians couldn't drink or eat from the Nile.

According to Scripture, despite the gravity of the situation, Pharaoh, after seeing his magicians perform some similar thing, turned around, went into his palace, *"and didn't take even this to heart."* This gruesome and intense scene had no impact on Pharaoh's hard unbelieving heart. This is a pattern we often see in Scripture regarding miracles. People see them, experience them, and are even in awe of them, but frequently, they aren't changed by them at all.

It is interesting to note that both the first miracle performed through Moses in Egypt and the first miracle performed by Jesus had to do with the transformation of water. In one case, water was turned into something gruesome and, in the other, into something gladsome. The transformation of water into blood on the banks of the Nile was a symbol of pain, suffering, and death. By contrast, when Jesus intervened at the wedding feast to transform water into wine, that miracle symbolized life, joy, hope, and rejuvenation.

Although Pharaoh saw the miracle in his day and failed to believe it, something very different happened at that wedding in Cana. John 2:11 says, *"Jesus did this, the first of his signs, in Cana of Galilee. He revealed his glory, and his disciples believed in him."* [50] On that night, in the midst of that happy moment, His disciples believed in Him. The most gruesome aspect of the Nile turning to blood is not smell, pain, suffering, or death. Rather, it's that even in the face of such an overwhelming miracle, Pharaoh remained unconvinced and did not believe. His heart only grew harder when it should have melted, submitted, and obeyed. The lesson here is

---

[50] John 2:11 (CSB)

that we don't want to face life with the unbelieving heart of Pharaoh but instead with the soft submissive heart of a disciple.

REFLECT—REFOCUS—REPENT—RESPOND

What did you hear God say today?

What will you do with what you learned?

What needs to change?

What questions do you still have?

What will you pray for?

RADICAL REPENTANCE

Matthew 27:54 (CSB) *"Truly this man was the Son of God!"*

Read Matthew 27:45–56

Salvation is indeed a miracle. Its miraculous nature is seen from many different angles. For example, we know that the Devil works to keep the lost engaged in spiritual blindness and far from God. The Apostle Paul said to the Corinthians, *"In their case, the god of this age has blinded the minds of the unbelievers to keep them from seeing the light of the gospel of the glory of Christ, who is the image of God."*[51] In John 3:19, Jesus says that humans are lovers of darkness. And in Ephesians 2, we are described as being *"dead"* in our trespasses. No matter how you look at it, the acceptance of God's salvation through Jesus Christ is miraculous. Salvation is never the result of our efforts; it is nothing less than the sovereign act of God in a person's life.

The crucifixion scene was one of chaos. There was crying, moaning, confusion, laughter, jeering, joking, and so much more happening, as Jesus and two criminals were left to suffer and die on the cross. Many were there that day, and many others passed by as the scene took place. Seven distinct miracles took place while Jesus was on the cross. The seventh was the radical repentance of this Roman centurion, who proclaimed, *"This man was the Son of God!"* What caused this battle-hardened Roman soldier to profess Christ as the Son of God? I believe the three things that brought him to repentance are the three things that still draw people to accept the gospel today.

First, what this centurion saw that day *challenged* him. As a Roman soldier, there is no doubt that his eyes had seen a great deal more than most men. His eyes had seen the world as he traveled with the army. His

---

[51] 2 Corinthians 4:4 (CSB)

eyes had witnessed the courage and cruelty of the battlefield. His vile eyes had likely been inside brothels and bars. His eyes had seen open fields that stretched to the horizon and large cities bustling with people. But what he saw on this day was unique. He saw Jesus lay His life down willingly on the cross. Jesus did not fight, beg, scream, or resist. This was not the first crucifixion this centurion's eyes had seen, but it was likely the first time he had seen an innocent man so willingly submit to the cruelty of the cross.

Next, what this centurion heard *confused* him. This Roman officer had heard many things during his lifetime. He had heard battle plans being formed. He had heard young men cry for their mothers as they faced their final moments of life on remote battlefields. He had heard the calm and stillness of the early morning at camp, and he had heard the battle cry of thousands on the eve of war. He had likely heard many on this day shout *"Crucify Him. Crucify Him. Crucify Him."* Then, he heard Jesus lovingly speak to His mother and John from the cross. Perhaps more importantly, he heard Jesus speak to him when he said, *"Father, forgive them, because they do not know what they are doing."*[52] What this centurion heard on this day confused him.

Finally, what he experienced on this day *changed* him. This soldier had experienced many things during his lifetime. But nothing in his vast experience could have prepared him for this day. As he attempted to reconcile everything he had seen and heard, the only possible explanation he was left with was *"Truly this man was the Son of God!"* How the angels in Heaven must have erupted in celebration (Luke 15:10) as this sinner recognized what even the most devout religious leaders standing near the cross on this day had failed to see, Jesus was the Messiah.

I am convinced that, even today, people are drawn to the gospel in the same way this soldier was. What they see, what they hear, and what they experience all have their effects. Much of what they see, hear, and

---

[52] Luke 23:34 (CSB)

experience comes from those who bear the name Christian. Do they see compassion? Do they hear forgiveness on our lips? Do they feel the love of Christ overflowing from our lives? Ultimately, the work of salvation is a sovereign act of God. He draws the lost unto Himself, but we must never forget that we play a part in the process. People are either seeing, hearing, and experiencing God through your life, or they are seeing, hearing, and experiencing something else. What will they see in you today? What will they see in you this week?

REFLECT—REFOCUS—REPENT—RESPOND

What did you hear God say today?

What will you do with what you learned?

What needs to change?

What questions do you still have?

What will you pray for?

WHIRLWIND OF WONDER

2 Kings 2:11 (CSB) —*Then Elijah went up into heaven in the whirlwind.*

Read 2 Kings 2:1–12

As a kid growing up in the extreme drought of the 1980s, I was no stranger to whirlwinds. While feeding the hogs, cleaning the barn, saddling the horses, or performing some other task on the ranch, it was not uncommon to experience a genuine South Texas whirlwind. Generally, my brothers, cousins, and I would scream *"whirlwind"* to alert everyone within earshot that it was time to have some fun. We would then excitedly rush toward this force of nature and run along as far as possible inside the middle of its fury. We would emerge with smiles on our filthy faces and completely covered in dust from head to toe. Tall tales of surviving the power of a tornado or subduing it would be told for the rest of the day.

Here, in 2 Kings, we find one of the most marvelous miracles in the entire Old Testament. Elijah is an aging prophet whose time on Earth was coming to an end. Everyone knew what was about to happen, and yet no-one seemed to know what was about to happen. Three times, Elijah encouraged his disciple Elisha to stay behind. Three times, Elisha refused by saying, *"As the Lord lives and as you yourself live, I will not leave you."* Three times others had said, *"Do you know that the Lord will take your master away from you today?"* All three times Elisha had responded by saying *"Yes, I know. Be quiet."* These were tense and strange times, as the great prophet Elijah took his final journey on Earth.

Elijah had been used by God in some of the mightiest and most miraculous ways ever recorded. He had been both the steward and vessel of God's grace for over two decades, and now his race was coming to an end. Naturally, everyone wondered what would happen next? Here, in 2 Kings 2:10, even Elijah acknowledged that he himself did not know what

SIGNS AND WONDERS

God's plans were for after his departure. All that was certain was that it was the end of an era.

Elijah is one of only two men we know of who never faced physical death. Fifty sons of the prophets followed at a distance as Elijah and Elisha walked together. Elijah struck the waters of Jordan, and they parted as he and Elisha walked across on dry ground. Then, these two men of God who had been inseparable were suddenly separated from one another by God. Elijah was miraculously taken up to Heaven in a whirlwind. This was his final day on Earth, but it would not be his final appearance in God's story.

John the Baptist's ministry was compared to Elijah in Luke 1:17. In John 1:21, John is forced to outright deny being Elijah. When Jesus asked his disciples who people said he was, some evidently thought he was none other than Elijah (Matthew 16:14, Mark 6:15). Then, Elijah, Moses, and Jesus are witnessed together in what is known as transfiguration (Matthew 17, Mark 9, and Luke 9). Although we can't be certain because the names of the two witnesses in Revelation 11:6 are not mentioned, most theologians believe the people in question are Moses and Elijah, whom God sends once again at this pivotal moment in history. After all, Malachi 4:5 proclaims, *"Look, I am going to send you the prophet Elijah before the great and terrible day of the Lord comes."*

Here, in this mighty whirlwind of wonder, this man of God vanished into eternity. Elisha and the others who witnessed it were left standing speechless and shocked by God's marvelous nature: *"As Elisha watched, he kept crying out, "My father, my father, the chariots and horsemen of Israel!""*[53]

There are many lessons we can learn from this whirlwind of wonder. First, it's clear that no matter whether we depart this world in a miraculous whirlwind or peacefully slip away in our sleep in the middle of the night, God's story continues, and we will continue to be a part of

---

[53] 2 Kings 2:12 (CSB)

it. Our departure may not be accompanied by the miraculous, but that doesn't make it any less of a miracle that we are granted adoption into the family of God and will, by the grace of God, continue our journey with Jesus for all eternity.

We are also assured through the life and departure of Elijah in this great whirlwind of wonder that even once we are gone, God's goodness will remain. Although many in Elijah's day wondered what would happen after this great prophet was gone, we have the benefit of hindsight. From here, we can clearly see that God continued to do great and marvelous things, even after this great and marvelous man was taken from our planet. This will be true for you and I as well. God's work will not end when our work is finished.

So, our hearts should be at peace as we await our own appointment with God's whirlwind of wonder. Like that blue-eyed blond-headed south Texas boy, may we run toward the whirlwind of God's grace with excited and expectant hearts.

SIGNS AND WONDERS

REFLECT—REFOCUS—REPENT—RESPOND

What did you hear God say today?

What will you do with what you learned?

What needs to change?

What questions do you still have?

What will you pray for?

CONFIDENT IN YOUR CALLING

2 Kings 2:14 (CSB) — *"Where is the Lord God of Elijah?"* he asked.

Read 2 Kings 2:11–18

If there's one thing I know for certain, it's this: the Devil loves to attack our calling in Christ. The attacks come from many different directions and are disguised in many different ways. However, one of the most effective attacks is an attack on our confidence. From those first moments Christ called your name, your confidence has been under attack. This is why so many joyfully surrender their lives to the call of Christ but fail to show up in full submission to be baptized in His name. It is precisely why so many start a ministry or emerge as great servants of the Master in the initial months of their newfound faith, only to fall away. Although many other examples could be offered, the source of the problem is frequently a loss of confidence in your calling.

Like all divine callings, Elisha's call was initiated by God. He was not looking to be called, nor was he in search of a new calling. Instead, the God of the universe, through His prophet Elijah, initiated this great calling on his life. 1 Kings 19:19 says that *"Elijah left there and found Elisha son of Shaphat as he was plowing. Twelve teams of oxen were in front of him, and he was with the twelfth team. Elijah walked by him and threw his mantle over him."*

Elisha was plowing a field when the call of God was placed on his life. He woke up that morning, ate his normal breakfast, got dressed, and went to work behind a team of oxen. Then, everything changed because he received a calling that he obeyed fully and immediately. He would faithfully follow Elijah for the remainder of his ministry, and then would have a long and distinguished ministry as a prophet himself.

As we discovered yesterday, many years later, Elijah was taken by the Lord in the presence of Elisha. Before this happened, Elisha's mentor Elijah had asked him a very important question. He said to Elisha, *"Tell me what I can do for you before I am taken from you."* To this, the younger prophet responded, *"Please, let me inherit two shares of your spirit."* In these words, we hear the echo of a man who was unsure of what was about to happen to him and what his own calling was. He wanted to inherit a double portion of the spirit that he had seen working all these years in his mentor. God, however, wanted to ignite a flame and pour out His spirit directly into the life of Elisha.

It's easy to see how Elisha would have been confused during this time of transition. To this point in his ministry, he had largely viewed his calling as one of support for Elijah. Who would he be when Elijah was gone and his role was no longer needed? The confidence he once felt that led him to say goodbye to his parents and slaughter his team of oxen all those years ago had eroded, and he was left to wonder who he was and what he would do without Elijah leading the way.

After the whirlwind whisked Elijah to Heaven, all that was left of him here on Earth was his cloak. When Elisha had been called all those years earlier, Elijah had thrown his cloak over Elisha while he was plowing. Now Elisha picked the prophet's cloak up from the ground and put it upon his own shoulders. No doubt, this brought some level of comfort and confidence to Elisha. As the earlier words of his mentor had expressed, *"You have asked for something difficult. If you see me being taken from you, you will have it. If not, you won't."*[54] Elisha had seen Elijah's miraculous departure and might have been emboldened by taking up his cloak. But would God use Him?

He walked back to the banks of the Jordan River, with fifty other sons of the prophets looking on from a distance. He took the cloak and struck the waters just as Elijah had done before and said, *"Where is the*

---

[54] 2 Kings 2:10 (CSB)

Lord God of Elijah?" And at that moment, the waters parted, and he walked across by himself on dry ground. Those watching understood the significance, and they came forth and confirmed his calling by bowing down on the ground before him. It was here that he found confidence in his calling and would go on to be a great prophet for the Lord.

Some might be tempted to think that the power that produced this miracle at the Jordan was the cloak of Elijah. This kind of thinking, however, is flawed. The miracle-working power of God was not in some old cloak; it was also not in the man who wore the cloak. The power belonged solely to the God these two men served and was only put on display as they followed His calling.

The same is true for you and I today. When we are living in obedience to Christ and His calling on our lives, we become the vessels of His wonder-working power. We are the hands and feet of Jesus in a dark, disturbing, deteriorating world. We don't have to perform signs and wonders in order to be used by God, but we must be obedient to our calling. When we lose confidence in our calling and forsake it, the Devil is pleased. If you have lost confidence in your calling, I pray that you would remove the cloak, strike the water today, and discover that the power of God is still alive and at work inside of you!

REFLECT—REFOCUS—REPENT—RESPOND

What did you hear God say today?

What will you do with what you learned?

What needs to change?

What questions do you still have?

What will you pray for?

THE MIRACLE OF ALL MIRACLES

John 20:18 (CSB) — *"I have seen the Lord!"*

Read John 20:1–18

It is impossible to do a study on the miracles of the Bible and not reflect on the miraculous resurrection of Jesus Christ. This is the crowning miracle of them all. If this miracle did not occur, then none did. When the angel gloriously declared, *"He is not here,"* the healing of humanity was assured, as the world learned that Jesus was indeed alive. His resurrection is mentioned almost one hundred and fifty times in Scripture. No matter how you look at it, the resurrection of Jesus is a very big deal.

Jesus would miraculously appear to His disciples and many others for a period of time before returning to His Father in the miraculous ascension. During these miraculous appearances, Jesus would perform additional signs and wonders to authenticate His claim on life and articulate His mission and purpose for the disciples. It was a glorious and confusing time to be sure; it was also exactly what the disciples needed to solidify their faith for what was to come.

The resurrection of Jesus makes your own resurrection possible. In speaking to Martha near the grave of her brother Lazarus, Jesus said, *"I am the resurrection and the life. The one who believes in me, even if he dies, will live. Everyone who lives and believes in me will never die. Do you believe this?"*[55] In John 6:39, Jesus says, *"This is the will of him who sent me: that I should lose none of those he has given me but should raise them up on the last day."* There is only one

---

[55] John 11:25–26 (CSB)

way to experience an eternal resurrection to life, and that is through Jesus Christ.

To the Romans, Paul writes, *"And if the Spirit of him who raised Jesus from the dead lives in you, then he who raised Christ from the dead will also bring your mortal bodies to life through his Spirit who lives in you."*[56] Paul also expressed his extreme confidence in the Church in Thessalonica, writing, *"For if we believe that Jesus died and rose again, in the same way, through Jesus, God will bring with him those who have fallen asleep."*[57] In the same way, 1 John 5:11–12 says it as plainly as it can be said, *"And this is the testimony: God has given us eternal life, and this life is in his Son. The one who has the Son has life. The one who does not have the Son of God does not have life."*

When Jesus' lifeless body was resurrected in that cold, dark, sealed tomb, so were you! I had the opportunity to witness the show titled *Jesus* at the Sights and Sound Theater in Branson, Missouri, in 2022. In the production, after Jesus is laid in the tomb and sealed, the guarded tomb is quiet for days. Suddenly, a light appears, and you are able to see inside. As you would expect, there is a lifeless body lying flat and dead still. Then, you see the chest of the actor draw in a large amount of air and immediately the actor sits up, stands up, and appears from the tomb. It is one of the most powerful things I have ever witnessed in my life. Not because I had not imagined this exact scene in my head thousands of times before but because for the first time as I sat there in my seat, I caught a glimpse of my own future resurrection.

The miracle of all miracles is not just that the Son of God is alive; it is that God, in His power, grace, and love, has chosen to allow all who call on the name of Jesus to experience this great resurrection power as well. The resurrection of Jesus was not a singular event that only impacted the life of Christ. It was a singular event that impacted the lives

---

[56] Romans 8:11 (CSB)

[57] 1 Thessalonians 4:14 (CSB)

of all believers. For it is precisely because of His resurrection that eternal life is possible for us.

This is nothing short of miraculous when you understand how wretched and rotten we all are. Paul correctly says of each of us, *"And you were dead in your trespasses and sins in which you previously walked according to the ways of this world, according to the ruler of the power of the air, the spirit now working in the disobedient. We too all previously lived among them in our fleshly desires, carrying out the inclinations of our flesh and thoughts, and we were by nature children under wrath as the others were also. But God, who is rich in mercy, because of his great love that he had for us, made us alive with Christ even though we were dead in trespasses. You are saved by grace! He also raised us up with him and seated us with him in the heavens in Christ Jesus, so that in the coming ages he might display the immeasurable riches of his grace through his kindness to us in Christ Jesus."*[58] Despite your sin, Jesus died for you, so you could experience a full and final eternal resurrection by trusting Him as your Lord and savior. This is the only way to find eternal life and experience divine resurrection power.

To Martha, Jesus asked the most important question of all. He asks each of us the same question, and in your answer to that question hangs eternity: *"Do you believe this?"* If you have yet to repent, confess, and believe, I can't urge you strongly enough to do so today. Below, you will find a simple prayer that you can pray right now. However, you shouldn't let your confession be the conclusion of your journey with Christ. If you chose to take this step of faith and believe, you should contact your pastor or small group leader and let them know what you have done. They will be overjoyed and ready to help you take your next steps on your journey as a follower of Jesus.

Prayer of repentance: Father, I come before you right now and confess that I am a sinner in need of your grace. I have fallen short and failed more times than I can count. I repent of my sins and, in faith, ask

---

[58] Ephesians 2:1–7 (CSB)

for your forgiveness. Thank you for loving me enough to send Jesus to die for my sins. Thank you for the undeserved grace and mercy I have received today. —Amen

REFLECT—REFOCUS—REPENT—RESPOND

What did you hear God say today?

What will you do with what you learned?

What needs to change?

What questions do you still have?

What will you pray for?

SIGNS AND WONDERS

THE MIRACLES OF GOD

WEEK NINE

WEEK NINE: SMALL GROUP CELEBRATION

Now that you have concluded this study, it's appropriate for your group to gather one final time to celebrate all that the Lord has done. Share a meal together and talk about the final five devotional readings from this week. Finally, I would strongly encourage you to discuss what your next topic of study will be. If your group has grown, it might be time to multiply. If your group has bonded and you still have some open chairs, it's time to consider what's next.

I know I've said this a few times already but thank you once again for taking part in this study. Thank you for taking the time to leave a five-star review of the study on Amazon. Thank you for connecting with me on social media and www.pastorpete.org. If you haven't done so already, let me invite you one final time to sign up for my *FREE* daily devotional podcast. Use the QR code below to sign up to have the podcast delivered to your email inbox every morning. May the Lord bless you in the most amazing ways as you continue your journey with Him.

Pastor Pete

Are you willing to take two minutes of your time and complete this short survey? Scan the QR code below or use the link to be directed to the online survey.

www.pastorpete.org/signs-wonders

If you would like to receive the Daily Devo podcast in your inbox each morning, scan the QR code in the image or visit www.pastorpete.org to sign up. Each morning, Pete shares a four minute devotion with believers from all around the world. Sign up today!

Dr. Pawelek regularly takes trips to the Holy Land and other spiritually significant locations. If you would like to be notified about future trips use the QR code in the image or visit www.pastorpete.org. Dr. Pawelek makes these trips as affordable as possible with the purchasing power of larger groups. By joining the email list you are *not* signing up for a trip, you are only asking to be notified when trips are planned.

APPENDIX A: BIBLICAL SIGNS AND WONDERS

OLD TESTAMENT MIRACLES

1. Creation: Genesis 1–2
2. Enoch's translation: Genesis 5:24
3. The flood of all creation: Genesis 7–8
4. Tower of Babel: Genesis 11:1–9
5. Smoking fire pot and flaming lamp: Genesis 15:17
6. Blinded Sodomites: Genesis 19:11
7. Destruction of Sodom and Gomorrah: Genesis 19:24–25
8. Lot's wife turned into a pillar of salt: Genesis 19:26
9. Miraculous conception of Isaac: Genesis 21:1–7
10. Elderly Sarah is supernaturally able to nurse Isaac: Genesis 21:7
11. Hagar's well: Genesis 21:14–21
12. Moses and the burning bush: Exodus 3
13. Moses' rod transformed into snake: Exodus 4:3–4, 30
14. Moses' hand transformed leprous: Exodus 4:6–7, 30
15. Aaron's rod transformed into a snake: Exodus 7:8–10
16. Nile River turned to blood: Exodus 7:20–25
17. Frogs: Exodus 8:1–15
18. Gnats: Exodus 8:16–19
19. Flies: Exodus 8:20–24
20. Death and disease in Egyptian livestock: Exodus 9:1–7
21. Boils: Exodus 9:8–12
22. Hail: Exodus 9:13–35
23. Locusts: Exodus 10:1–20
24. Darkness over the land: Exodus 10:21–23
25. Death of firstborn: Exodus 12:29–30
26. The Pillar of God's presence: Exodus 13:21–22; 14:19–20
27. Miracle of protection: Exodus 14:19–20
28. Dry ground crossing of the Red Sea: Exodus 14:21–31
29. Destruction of Pharaoh's army: Exodus 14:23–28
30. Bitter water turned sweet: Exodus 15:23–25

31. Quail from Heaven: Exodus 16:13, Numbers 11:31–32
32. Manna from Heaven: Exodus 16:14–35
33. Water from the rock: Exodus 17:5–8
34. Defeat of Amalek: Exodus 17:9–13
35. Strange fire on Aaron's sacrifice: Leviticus 9:24
36. The destruction of Nadab and Abihu: Leviticus 10:1–2
37. Judgment by fire: Numbers 11:1–3
38. Miriam's leprosy: Numbers 12:10–15
39. Earth swallowed Korah: Numbers 16:32–34
40. 250 men consumed by fire: Numbers 16:35–45
41. Plague destroyed murmurers: Numbers 16:41:50
42. Aaron's rod sprouts: Numbers 17:1–11
43. Water from the rock at Kadesh: Numbers 20:8–11
44. God sends poisonous snakes to the camp: Numbers 21:6
45. God heals camp with bronze snake: Numbers 21:5–9
46. Balaam's donkey speaks: Numbers 22:21–35
47. The Jordan River is parted: Joshua 3:14–17
48. Walls of Jericho: Joshua 6:6–20
49. The miracle of defeat at Ai: Joshua 7–8
50. Victory by hailstorm: Joshua 10:9–11
51. Sun and moon stand still: Joshua 10:12–14
52. The miracle of leadership and peace under Othniel: Judges 3:9–11
53. Gideon's fleece: Judges 6:36–40
54. Angel in the fire: Judges 13:20
55. Samson kills a lion: Judges 14:5–6
56. Samson kills Philistines: Judges 14:19
57. Samson's provision: Judges 15:19
58. Samson and the city gates: Judges 16:3
59. Dagon's house destroyed by Samson: Judges 16:29–30
60. Birth of Samuel: 1 Samuel 1
61. Dagon's idol destroyed: 1 Samuel 5:1–12
62. Disease on the Philistines: 1 Samuel 5:1–12
63. Men of Beth-shemesh destroyed: 1 Samuel 6:19–20
64. Supernatural thunder: 1 Samuel 7:10–12
65. Thunder and rain at harvest: 1 Samuel 12:18
66. Goliath defeated by David: 1 Samuel 17
67. Supernatural sound: 2 Samuel 5:23–25
68. Uzzah's death: 2 Samuel 6:6–7
69. Miracle of wisdom and a receptive heart Solomon: 1 Kings 3:9

70. Jeroboam's hand withered and healed: 1 Kings 13:4–6
71. Destruction of altar at Bethel: 1 Kings 13:4–6
72. Prophet killed: 1 Kings 13:1–26
73. Drought ordered by Elijah: 1 Kings 17:1
74. Elijah fed by ravens: 1 Kings 17:4–6
75. Widows jug and jar: 1 Kings 17:12–16
76. Widow's son raised to life: 1 Kings 17:17–24
77. Sacrifice consumed by fire: 1 Kings 18:19–40
78. Rain: 1 Kings 18:41–45
79. Destruction by command of fire: 2 Kings 1:9–12
80. Jordan parted: 2 Kings 2:8
81. Elijah taken to Heaven: 2 Kings 2:11
82. Jordan River parted by Elisha: 2 Kings 2:14
83. Waters of Jericho healed: 2 Kings 2:20–22
84. Mockers destroyed by bears: 2 Kings 2:24
85. Water supplied for Jehoshaphat: 2 Kings 3:16–20
86. Widow's oil multiplied: 2 Kings 4:1–7
87. Shunammite's son raised to live: 2 Kings 4:19–37
88. Poisoned pottage of no effect: 2 Kings 4:38–41
89. 20 loaves feed one hundred: 2 Kings 4:42–44
90. Naaman cured of leprosy: 2 Kings 5:10–14
91. Gehazi struck with leprosy: 2 Kings 5:15–27
92. Axe-head floats: 2 Kings 6:5–7
93. Ben-Hadad's plans revealed: 2 Kings 6:8–17
94. Syrian army goes blind: 2 Kings 6:18
95. Syrian army healed of blindness: 2 Kings 6:20
96. Syrian army defeated: 2 Kings 6:18–20
97. Life in Elisha's bones: 2 Kings 13:21
98. Mass death: 2 Kings 19:35
99. Sun moves backwards: 2 Kings 20:9–11
100. Uzziah's leprosy: 2 Chronicles 26:16–21
101. The miracle of God's providence: Book of Esther
102. Protection in the fire: Daniel 6:16–23
103. The storm of the Lord: Jonah 1:4
104. Jonah discovered by casting lots: Jonah 1:7–8
105. Jonah in the belly of a fish: Jonah 2:1–10
106. Revival of Nineveh: Jonah 3:1–10
107. The east wind: Jonah 4:8–10

SIGNS AND WONDERS

NEW TESTAMENT

1. Conception of John the Baptist: Luke 1:5–24
2. Virgin Birth of Christ: Luke 1:26–35
3. Star of Bethlehem: Matthew 2:1–12
4. Water to wine: John 2:1–11
5. Child healed in Cana: John 4:46–54
6. Demoniac healed in Capernaum synagogue: Mark 1:23–26
7. Peter's mother-in-law healed: Matthew 8:14–17
8. Mass healings: Luke 4:40–41, Matthew 8:16–17, Mark 1:32–34
9. Miraculous catch of fish: Luke 5:1–11
10. Leper healed at Capernaum: Matthew 8:1–4, Mark 1:40–45, Luke 5:12–15
11. Paralytic healed in Capernaum: Matthew 9:1–8
12. The healing of an impotent man: John 5:1–9
13. Centurion's servant healed: Matthew 8:5–13, Luke 7:1–10
14. Withered hand restored: Matthew 12:9–14, Luke 6:6–10, Mark 3:1–6
15. Widow's son raised to life: Luke 7:11–18
16. Demoniac healed in Galilee: Matthew 12:22–23
17. Jesus calms the storm: Luke 8:22–25, Matthew 8:23–27, Mark 4:35–41
18. Demon-possessed men healed: Matthew 8:28–34, Luke 8:26–27, Mark 5:1–20
19. Jairus' daughter raised to life: Matthew 9:23
20. Woman with issue of blood healed: Matthew 9:20–22
21. Blind receive sight: Matthew 9:27–31
22. Dumb spirit cast out: Matthew 9:32–33
23. Feeding of 5000: Matthew 14:13–21, Mark 6:31–44, Luke 9:10–17, John 6:1–14
24. Walking on water: Matthew 14:22–36, Mark 6:45–54, John 6:15–21
25. Syrophoenician daughter healed: Matthew 15:21–28, Mark 7:24–30
26. Deaf and dumb man healed: Mark 7:31–37
27. Feeding of the 4000: Matthew 15:30–38, Mark 8:1–9
28. Transfiguration of Christ: Matthew 17:24–27
29. Coin in fish's mouth: Matthew 17:27
30. Deaf and dumb man healed: Mark 7:31–37

31. Blind man healed: Mark 8:22–26
32. Devil cast out of child: Mark 9:14–29
33. Man born blind healed: John 9
34. Ten lepers healed: Luke 17:11–19
35. Jesus heals woman with physical disability: Luke 13:10–17
36. Man with edema cured: Luke 14:1–6
37. Lazarus raised to life: John 11:1–46
38. Blind Bartimaeus: Matthew 20:29–34, Mark 10:46–52, Luke 18:35–43
39. Withered fig tree: Matthew 21:17–22, Mark 11:12–24
40. Malchus' ear healed: Matthew 26:51–56, Mark 14:46–47, Luke 22:50–51, John 18:10–11
41. Second miraculous catch of fish: John 21:1–14
42. The miracle of darkness: Matthew 27:45–49
43. The miracle of divine separation: Matthew 27:46–50
44. The miracle of the torn curtain: Matthew 27:51
45. The miracle of the earthquake and opened tombs: Matthew 27:51–53
46. The miracle of Jesus' resurrection: Matthew 28:1–10, Mark 16:1–11, Luke 24:1–12, John 20:1–18
47. Pentecost: Acts 2:1–14
48. Lame man healed by Peter: Acts 3:6
49. Death of Ananias and Sapphira: Acts 5:5–10
50. Numerous signs and wonders; Peter's shadow: Acts 5:12–16
51. Sick healed by Peter: Acts 5:15
52. Apostles freed from prison with the help of angel: Acts 5:19
53. Stephen's miracles: Acts 6:8
54. Stephen's vision of Jesus: Acts 7:55–56
55. Philip cast out demonic spirits: Acts 8:6–13
56. Christ's appearance to Saul: Acts 9:1–5
57. Ananias' vision: Acts 9:10
58. Paul regains his sight: Acts 9:17–18
59. Aeneas healed by Peter- Acts 9:32-35
60. Dorcas raised to life: Acts 9:36–42
61. Cornelius's vision: Acts 10:9–20
62. Peter's vision: Acts 10:9–20
63. Peter released from prison with the help of angel: Acts 12:7–11
64. Elymas blinded: Acts 13:11
65. Paul heals lame man: Acts 14:1–18

66. Miracle of Paul's recovery: Acts 14:19–28
67. Paul's vision for Macedonia: Acts 16:9
68. Paul and Silas released from prison by earthquake: Acts 16:25–26
69. Numerous miracles performed through Paul: Acts 19:11–18
70. Eutychus restored to life: Acts 20:10
71. Paul unaffected by snake bite: Acts 28:5
72. Publius' father healed: Acts 28:8
73. John's vision on Patmos and the book of Revelation. Numerous miracles are outlined and foretold in this book about what is to come.
74. There are without a doubt innumerable other miracles performed by Christ and in the early Church that were witnessed but not recorded in Scripture: John 20:30, Acts 10:38–39.

ADDITIONAL NEW TESTAMENT MIRACLES:

Some count the eleven post-resurrection appearances of Christ as miraculous events. I have chosen to leave these off my list primarily because they only firmly meet the standard of *three* of my four defining questions to identify the miraculous. In my judgment, the question to which these events fall shy of is "Does the event's overall purpose reveal the person and purpose of Jesus Christ, or the power, nature, or Glory of God?" In my opinion, the purpose and person of Jesus Christ was already known to those Christ appeared to in these supernatural events. While a case could be made that these events *do* reveal the power, nature, or Glory of God, I felt that they fell short of my personal standard in this regard. Having said that, while I left them off my official list of miracles, I wouldn't criticize anyone who might include them on theirs.

1. Christ's appearance to Mary Magdalene: Mark 16:9
2. Christ's appearance to other women: Matthew 28:9
3. Christ's appearance to two disciples: Luke 24:15–31
4. Christ's appearance to 10 disciples: John 20:19–24
5. Christ's appearance to 11 disciples: John 20:26–28
6. Christ's appearance while disciples are fishing: John 21:1–24
7. Christ's appearance to disciples in Galilee: Matthew 28:16–17
8. Christ's appearance to Peter: 1 Corinthians 15:5
9. Christ's appearance to over 500 people: 1 Corinthians 15:6
10. Christ's appearance to James: 1 Corinthians 15:7
11. Christ's appearance and ascension: Acts 1:2–9

Made in the USA
Las Vegas, NV
15 September 2022